Robespierre and the French Revolution

France at the end of the eighteenth century was a world of great political unrest, a veritable seed-bed of democracy and socialism, where revolution was the order of the day. Into this chaotic atmosphere came Maximilien Robespierre, a man of humble origin whose social and political ideas were inevitably to change the history of France.

In these pages, J. M. Thompson, one of the world's leading authorities on the history of the French Revolution, brings to life the man and his part in the movement. Here you see Robespierre as he outmaneuvers the great Mirabeau, becomes the champion of the Paris Commune, initiates a new social order, and helps create the first French Republic. And you see him again as he sends thousands of Frenchmen to their deaths on the guillotine and eventually becomes himself its prize victim.

A compact and scholarly study, this book provides a twentieth-century look at one of the most dramatic and critical periods in history.

Robespierre and the French Revolution

J. M. THOMPSON, F.B.A., F.R. Hist. S.
Honorary Fellow at Magdalen College

COLLIER BOOKS

FIRST COLLIER BOOKS EDITION 1962
SIXTH PRINTING 1969

Robespierre and the French Revolution was published in a hardcover edition by The Macmillan Company

This title first appeared as a volume in the Teach Yourself History series under the general editorship of A. L. Rowse

The Macmillan Company

Printed in the United States of America

Contents

Robespierre and the French Revolution

Prologue

WHY ROBESPIERRE? Why not rather Sieyès, the architect and constitutionalist of the National Assembly? Why not Mirabeau, its foremost orator and statesman, the enemy of despotism and feudalism, the champion of a limited monarchy? Or Danton, the inspirer of national resistance to foreign invasion and of reaction against republican despotism? Or Lafayette, the hero of American independence, the commander of the National Guard, the guardian of the Constitution?

Robespierre was a provincial lawyer whose orbit never moved outside Artois and Paris. He had none of Mirabeau's experience of men and affairs, of his fierce vitality, or impulsive eloquence. A deputy from the country with a provincial accent and a mean appearance, he made little figure in the early sessions of the States-general; most of his speeches in the Convention were carefully prepared harangues, more suitable for the lecturer's desk or the preacher's pulpit than for the tribune of a popular assembly. He could never extemporise an appeal to the crowd, like Danton. There was none of Lafayette's glamour, nothing heroic or soldierly in his spectacled eyes and sharp features. He was made for opposition, not government. His gift was not that of Sieyès for political or constitutional science, but for the arts of criticism and party intrigue. Nevertheless, after working his way up, with infinite study and pertinacity, from back-bench obscurity, he rode in turn every wave of popular reaction to the political wind of the moment, and made himself the spokesman of that Parisian and provincial lower middle class (*petite bourgeoisie*) which the earthquake of the Revolution had intruded into the twisted strata of French society. It was not his fault that the country was forced into a war that dragged the King from his throne, and necessitated a republican regime of centralised control and intimidation. It was never his wish to be the figure-head

9

of a despotic committee government. He was led, not by cruel ambition but by common hopes and fears, into the bloodshed of the Reign of Terror.

But from first to last the weakness of Robespierre illustrated and impersonated the strength of the Revolution: as a supporter of Mirabeau's policy in 1789, as a visionary champion of popular liberty in 1790, as a cautious republican in 1791, as an opponent of war and a partisan of the Paris Commune in 1792, as the chief exponent of Jacobinism in 1793, and as its most prominent martyr in 1794. No one else had lived so fully through every experience of the Revolution or with such a fastidious regard for its first principles. Mirabeau and Danton were dead, Sieyès was living in retirement, Lafayette lay in a foreign prison; when Robespierre fell, it was the end of the first phase of a movement which was indeed destined to repeat more than once its round from monarchy to republicanism and back again; but there would not be another Robespierre.

Across the Channel, where the events in France were followed at first with sympathy, then with disgust, and finally with apprehension, only two names forced themselves on public attention; and they were both names of persons who were not typical Frenchmen and who never set foot on British soil. The events of 1789–94 meant, for most Englishmen, Robespierre and the Reign of Terror; the events of 1796–1815, Bonaparte and the conquest of Europe. In France itself only these two names have been given to a society and to a magazine devoted to the history of their epochs. Both were self-made men, of small origins, laborious and ambitious, who had to make their way in a hostile world: Robespierre from within, with mole-like progress from point to point; Bonaparte from without, with an eagle flight that envisaged world-vistas and world-problems. One rose and fell within the small circuit of Paris and the concentrated events of five years; the other rose and fell by policies and campaigns of fifteen years that covered all Europe from Paris to Moscow and from the Atlantic to the Indian Ocean.

Yet in terms of territory (and territory dear to France) it may be said that Robespierre won the Rhine frontier and Napoleon lost it; and in terms of achievement that the work of the Empire would have been impossible unless it had been built upon that of the Republic. In the final judgment of history, the events of the five years are likely to be accounted as of more lasting value than those of the fifteen; and to Robespierre may be attributed a greatness due to his setting and his theme which is not incomparable with that which Napoleon claims by his own genius of thought and act.

Chapter 1

1789

ON MAY 10, 1774, in a corner of his huge palace at Versailles, Louis XV died miserably of smallpox—that great leveller, which in the eighteenth century spared neither sage nor beauty, peasant nor king. He was not a very old man, but he had been fifty-nine years on the Bourbon throne; and that half century had seen more changes in French society and ideas than State and Church could any longer control. It was—if there ever was one—an era of transition; a tired age was dying, and men predicted hopefully that a new age was being born: a golden age of Reason and Philanthropy, of Prosperity and Progress. The new king, in whom these hopes were bound up—for all Frenchmen were monarchists at heart—was a shy, undignified youth of twenty, married four years ago to an Austrian princess a year younger than himself, who might have captivated Parisian society by her charm and high spirits if she had not been unfairly charged with the sin of failing to produce an heir to the throne.

Louis XVI was, indeed, quite unfit to lead his country into the promised land. But he had been well advised in his choice of ministers: Vergennes, the ablest diplomatist of the day, for the Foreign Office; Malesherbes, a philanthropic reformer, as Home Secretary; Turgot, a famous economist and provincial administrator, as Minister of Finance; and as pilot and ballast for the ship of State, Maurepas, an "elder statesman" whose memories went back to the early days of the last reign, when the old King was still Louis *le Bien-aimé* and the old orthodoxies were still undisturbed by Montesquieu or Beccaria, Rousseau or Voltaire. The crowning of Louis and Marie Antoinette at Rheims in 1775, carried out with all the traditional magnificence, was almost an acclamation of philosophy upon the throne.

On their return from Rheims, the new sovereigns paid the customary visit to the *Collège* (we should say, School) of Louis-le-Grand in Paris, where a Latin speech of welcome was delivered by the brightest classical scholar of his year, a poor orphan of seventeen from Arras, named Maximilien de Robespierre. They were to meet again when Louis was on his trial before the National Convention in December 1792 and Robespierre clamoured for his death.

In the age-long constitution of French society, so soon to be dissolved by revolution, the privileged orders of Clergy and Nobility and the unprivileged but financially and professionally important *bourgeoisie*—corresponding to our middle classes—formed no more than a thin crust upon the surface of the workers: half a million privileged and a million *bourgeois,* or thereabouts, to twenty-five million workers, nine-tenths of them agricultural. But in the few great cities (Paris had a population of about 600,-000, and some half a dozen ports or manufacturing centres approached six figures), and in the many county towns, as we should call them, the dignitaries of the cathedral, the parish priests, the members of the Town Council (*municipalité*), the magistrates, lawyers, and solicitors, and all the minor officials of civil and ecclesiastical government more than held their own. The sons of the *petite bourgeoisie,* if they found no vocation in the Church, and had no family business to inherit, cherished two ambitions: to own a plot of land and to secure a legal or official oppointment. The first carried by custom the right to put *de* before one's name (in truth it was little more than the dubious transition from "Mr." to "Esq." which causes us so much embarrassment); the second stood for social consideration and a fixed income, however small.

Arras was such a county town and the Robespierres such a family. They had lived in that part of the country for three hundred years, and if Maximilien inherited something of a foreign streak in his character (he was sometimes accused of being an Irishman), it must have come from a remote ancestor. He kept the *de* in his signature until the Revolution turned all Frenchmen into "citizens" (*citoyens*)—kept it even when as Secretary of the Assembly he signed the decree abolishing titles of nobility; and he always dressed as a gentleman of the old regime, with powdered hair, a smart coat, and a high stock. Yet, in fact, in 1789, at the age of thirty-one, he was almost a nobody: an orphan, for his mother was dead and his father had deserted the home; with a younger brother and sister upon his hands; with a brilliant school career behind him, a small and unremunerative legal practice, and a reputation for advanced opinions which did him no good with the ecclesiastics who had paid for his education or the lawyers who might have found him rich clients. He was admitted to have a talent for forensic oratory and essay-writing—the readiest approach in those days to a public career; and even Paris heard of him when he defended a certain M. Vissery against the benighted citizens of Saint-Omer on the charge of endangering their lives by erecting one of Mr. Franklin's new-fangled lightning-conductors. But he had attacked the practices of the Arras courts; he had expressed detestation of capital punishment; and he had appealed to Louis XVI to come forward as the heaven-sent champion of the rights of the common people.

Robespierre was not alone in his predicament. At school he had read Voltaire, Raynal, and Rousseau, and had discussed irreligion and enlightenment with Camille Desmoulins, Stanislas Fréron, and other clever students who were afterwards leaders of the Revolution. All over France there were young men growing up with the same disrespect for authority in Church and State, the same belief that science and reason could inaugurate a brave new world, the same ambition to find a way to Paris and set the Seine on fire. When the States-general met in 1789, it was realised that the great majority of the deputies of the Third Estate were provincial lawyers of one kind or another, and many of them belonged to Robespierre's generation. In the National Convention of 1792 nearly one deputy out of four had been born within two years of his birthday in 1758. To these men the outbreak of the Revolution in 1789 was like the first breaking of the frost at the end of an arctic winter: flowers sprang from the ground and living creatures awoke from sleep. A new world was before them—to explore and to exploit; at once a country to be saved and a career to be made.

Robespierre may not have realised more than a few of the causes of the French Revolution enumerated by modern historians. Different men approached the crisis from different sides. Some aspects of the situation would have been so familiar as to be taken for granted: the decline of the Monarchy during Louis XV's long reign; the weakening of the position of the Church; the transference of wealth and social consequence from the nobility and gentry to the commercial and professional middle class; or the continual rise in prices which prevented the workers from profiting by the increasing prosperity of the country. In Robespierre's legal outlook the most important issue was that raised by the contest between the King and the *parlements*—those Appeal Courts in Paris and certain provincial cities which in the long absence of parliamentary government had acquired the right to register and so to give legal currency to the legislative decrees of the crown. This contest, which had already broken out during the later years of the last reign, had been renewed when Louis XVI's Finance Minister, Brienne, tried to break the resistance of the *parlements* to the imposition of new taxes by suspending their members from their duties and entrusting their power of registration to wholly new courts. It stood to reason that all lawyers, even reforming lawyers like Robespierre, would object to this measure; what Brienne did not foresee was that their opposition would be supported by the clergy, their traditional enemies, and by their traditional victims, the People—a word which meant in effect the opinion of Paris (for the provinces either had no opinion or echoed that of the capital); and Paris, though it disliked lawyers, regarded the legislative "veto" of the *parlements* as a bulwark of popular liberty. This public opposition took the form of a demand for the summoning of the States-general (*états-généraux*), or Parliament of France, in its three Houses of Clergy, Nobility, and Commons (*tiers état*), which had not met since the time of Henri IV, 175 years ago.

To the flood of political writings in which this proposal was welcomed and discussed, Robespierre contributed a pamphlet addressed to the people of Artois. Though he had offended the clergy and antagonised the lawyers, he was sufficiently well known in his native town of Arras to fancy himself as a candidate for election to the States-general. He had lived there all his life, first with his parents, then with the uncle who became his guardian. Now his own householder, with his sister and young brother, in the respectable rue des Rapporteurs (the house, rebuilt, still stands and bears his name), he could entertain his friends at the bar, and the fellow-members of the Rosati, a literary dining club, or of the local *Académie des belles-lettres,* amongst whom he was known as an essayist and versifier of no common merit. His legal practice, too, had brought him into touch with poor clients who appreciated his radical views; and he believed that they would vote for him. His pamphlet, *A la nation artésienne,* was therefore no abstract essay on liberty, equality, and fraternity, but a summing-up of all the local grievances, with the conclusion that the only remedy for them lay in the election of persons like himself as deputies to the new Parliament. And when he was elected, fifth in a list of eight "representatives of the Third Estate of Artois," he carried with him to Versailles, where the deputies were summoned to meet the King, an Address (*cahier*) containing, along with their credentials, a long list of the grievances (*doléances*) of the professional men, tradesmen, and workers of the town who had elected them, together with suggested reforms. Such *cahiers,* carried to Versailles from all parts of France by the 600 deputies of the *tiers état,* contributed more to the Revolution than the political theories of the intelligentsia, and are the most valuable evidence for the state of the country in 1789.

When, in January of that year, Necker, a rich Swiss financier whom the King had in desperation called from his bank counter to be Controller-General of Finance (an office which was in effect that of Prime Minister), issued the regulations for election to the States-general, it was found that he had accepted the view forced upon him by common justice and public opinion that the Third Estate —the "unprivileged" *bourgeoisie* and workers; in other words, some 98 per cent. of the population—should, at any rate, have as many representatives as the remaining 2 per cent.—the two "privileged" Orders taken together. Accordingly, at the royal reception of delegates on May 2, in the procession through the streets of Versailles on May 4, and at the opening session of May 5, the French nation was represented by 300 deputies elected by the Clergy, 300 by the Nobility, and 600 by the Commons. Robespierre and his colleagues, travelling by coach from Arras (he was so poor that he had to borrow his fare), were barely in time for these opening ceremonies, whose feudal magnificence seemed to the Commoners, in their uncomfortable medieval costumes, as meaningless as a modern pageant. But the interminable meeting of May 5 must have left upon his shrewd mind the same impression as upon that of the big, ugly man upon a neighbouring bench at whom everybody pointed as a renegade noble, with an unequalled reputation for ability and immorality —the Comte de Mirabeau. For the non-committal speech of the King, Barentin's almost inaudible warning against dangerous innovations, and Necker's tedious figures of finance, left the real issues unanswered. Would the Assembly be allowed to vote taxes or to propose constitutional reforms? Would the Third Estate be able to use their numbers, if need be, to outvote the Clergy and Nobility? Was there any real intention to consult the nation, or only a pretence of it, to cover new acts of royal absolutism, prompted by the Queen, the court, and the ministers of the crown?

With a unanimous hostility and self-control that the Government had never expected, the Third Estate, for a month after their first meeting, refused to transact any business until the two orders should unite with them to form a genuine Parliament. They knew that they had friends amongst the clergy—for many parish priests shared their views—and they felt that Paris opinion was rising in their favour. Robespierre, in a maiden speech on May 16, proposed that the clergy should be invited to join them; and though nothing came of it, he was honoured by the support of Mirabeau, and was soon converted from suspicion to admiration of "the Devil's Disciple." He intervened again on June 6 with an impromptu attack upon the Archbishop of Nîmes, who had suggested a conference on Poor Relief: "Let the bishops [he cried] renounce a luxury which is an offence to Christian humility; let them sell their coaches and horses, and give to the poor." This outburst caused a sensation and the speaker's name went round the House; but Robespierre was a little alarmed at his own verbosity, and seldom spoke again without a manuscript in his hands. He was ambitious; he was self-confident; but he feared to compromise his career by premature moves. He must cultivate the right people and support the causes that were going to win in the long run. So we find him getting an introduction to Necker, and meeting Necker's ugly but clever daughter, Mme de Staël, who thought him an honest retailer of second-hand opinions. But what young Radical was ever otherwise?

At any rate, he was by now making a name in the Assembly as one of the most prominent spokesmen of the Left. It was not merely later partisanship that induced David to represent him in the foreground of his famous picture of the Tennis-court Oath (June 20)—when the "National Assembly" (self-styled three days before) defied the King to dissolve it—pressing both hands upon his breast, "as though he had two hearts for liberty". It was not by accident that he was one of those chosen out of the 600 to accompany the King to Paris on July 17, after the fall of the Bastille on the 14th, and declared that "the image of this great event—the surrender of the crown to the people—was engraved for ever on the hearts of all who witnessed it." His speeches in the Assembly show him increasingly an enemy of the throne and a champion of abstract rights—liberty of possession, liberty of conscience, liberty of opinion—such as were embodied in the first clauses of the Rights of Man (August 20).

In the crucial constitutional question of the legislative powers of the crown, he was the spokesman of the Artois and Breton deputies (the leading representatives of the Left) who wished to abolish absolutely the royal veto. When the King tried to avoid signing the decrees of August 4—the "abolition of feudalism"—it was Robespierre who persuaded the House to insist on his compliance. It was he who reduced the King's Civil List (as we should call it) to an annual grant, and moved for the unconditional release of all prisoners under *lettres de cachet*—arbitrary warrants of arrest issued by the crown. In two of these matters, at least, he was now against Mirabeau, who was becoming alarmed at the Assembly's hostility to the Government, and feared that it might be impossible to save enough from the wreck of royal prerogative to preserve even a limited monarchy. The issue between monarchy and republic was, in fact, already beginning to appear. Robespierre was not a republican; but the failure of Mirabeau's policy was the first step towards the success of Robespierre's.

Chapter 2

The New Order

PARIS, WITH ITS half million of merchants, tradesmen, lawyers, officials, journalists, students, shopkeepers, artisans, and labourers; Paris, with its sumptuous *hôtels*, towering *appartements*, and teeming tenements; Paris, the walled enclosures of whose palace-gardens and nunneries overshadowed narrow cobbled streets where dirt and smells dimmed the sunlight; Paris, with its royal, municipal, and popular centres in the Tuileries, the Hôtel de Ville, and the Palais-Royal; Paris, whose citizens, prouder of their capital than of their country, and certain of its right to dictate the art and literature and government of France, had their own view of what was going on at Versailles and their own solution of the crisis: this Paris would take charge of the Revolution.

On July 14 the Parisians of the East end (*faubourg Saint-Antoine*), hearing that the King had dismissed the popular Necker and believing that he was mobilising troops to overawe the Assembly and occupy the capital, had seized arms from the Invalides (the Chelsea Hospital of Paris) and, aided by mutineers of the French Guard, had compelled the surrender of the garrison in the Bastille; the electors of the city's Third Estate deputies had thereupon taken over the municipal government, formed a National Guard to keep order, and in effect set Paris in a state of armed insurrection against the King. Louis' visit to Paris three days later sanctioned this state of affairs, and the first phase of the Revolution was over.

But Louis and his advisers were only waiting for another opportunity to strike. Within two months fresh troops gathered at Versailles—foreign mercenaries, upon whom alone now the King could depend—and a royalist banquet in the palace coincided with an ominous shortage of bread in the capital. On October 5 a mob of housewives and market-women marched out to Versailles to demand food, and stayed to invade the palace and endanger the life of the Queen. The next day Louis, who had thought of flight, was persuaded to accompany the demonstrators back to Paris, and the royal family became, for nearly three years, practically prisoners in the Tuileries. The States-general, now (since June) converted into the National or Constituent Assembly (*assemblée nationale, constituante*)—a single-chamber Parliament with power to make a constitution—followed the King, and soon continued its meetings in the royal riding-school (*manège*) on the north side of the Tuileries gardens.

This removal of the seat of government from Versailles to Paris had momentous effects upon the character and course of the Revolution and no little influence upon the life of Robespierre. It was as though our Revolution of 1688 had been marked by a compulsory transference of the royal family from Windsor to Westminster; but with the essential difference that for nearly two centuries the French Windsor had been the seat of an absolute monarchy to which no power in the State could offer serious resistance, and the French Westminster had seen no Parliament, nor any symbol of representative government. The Bourbons had ruled by virtue of their personal wealth, their patronage of the nobility, their disposal of ecclesiastical offices, their provincial governors (*intendants*), their control over the judges and magistrates, and their command of the army. Now the King was the salaried figure-head (Robespierre called him the *premier commis,* or senior clerk) of the State; the nobility had lost their titles and a great part of their estates; the bishops and clergy were soon to be appointed by popular election; the *intendants* would be replaced by a hierarchy of committees; judges and magistrates would be elected like national and local deputies; and the royal army was so disaffected that the King could only count on a few foreign regiments; whilst the *Garde Nationale* now being set on foot all over the country was in effect a Home

Guard of two million men, its loyalty pledged to the New Order, whatever that might turn out to be.

Let it not be thought that this last phrase misrepresents the mentality of 1789. Most revolutions are led by talkative idealists—the editor of a *Clarion* or the author of a *Revolutionalist's Handbook*. But the force of the movement comes from the rank and file, who dumbly feel that the present regime is intolerable and that any change must be for the better. The *cahiers* of 1789, which had been definite enough about the grievances of cobblers or shopkeepers and the abuses of the courts, the landlords, and the tax-collectors, were unanimously vague as to the "rights" which they claimed and the "constitution" under which they hoped to secure them. The Declaration of Rights had now (since August) defined Liberty and Equality in terms that satisfied the philosopher; but the man in the street soon found that his liberty was hampered by the liberty of his neighbour, and that equality only meant the privilege of taxing oneself, sending oneself to prison, or sacrificing one's life for a cause that was no longer one's own. The unconsidered People would put up with this so long as the Revolution freed them from their obligations to their landlords and their fears of forced labour, tithes, salt taxes, and the other injustices of the old regime, and so long as it added acres to the countryman's holdings of land or put more money into the labourer's pocket. As for the professional men, merchants, and intellectuals who controlled the Assembly, they were finding easier profits and better-paid jobs under the new Government than the old. It was evidently to their interest to keep political power in their own hands, to legislate so far as feasible in the interests of trade, property, and middle-class security. But they always had in their memories the eighteenth-century experience of peasant revolts in the countryside and bread riots in the towns; always an uneasy suspicion of what might be brewing in the clubs and cafés, the sectional meetings and popular societies of an unfamiliar and inscrutable capital.

Robespierre was not afraid of Paris, as were so many deputies of the Right, some 200 of whom resigned their seats when the Assembly moved to the capital. His anti-monarchical leanings made him popular amongst the *habitués* of the cafés and the loungers of the Palais-Royal —the old residence of the Duc d'Orléans, recently turned into a garden and a colonnade, with shops, restaurants, and gambling-hells—where Desmoulins had started the movement that led to the fall of the Bastille, and where every rumour to the discredit of the King and the ministers had its origin. But he had no gifts of a demagogue, as Danton had, or Pétion. He lived quietly in the respectable *Marais* —the Bloomsbury of Paris—and walked daily to the *manège,* often with a speech in his pocket; or to the new *Society of Friends of the Constitution,* nicknamed, from its premises in the old Dominican monastery in the rue Saint-Honoré, the Jacobin Club.

This was a successor to the smaller Breton Club at Versailles, where the Breton deputies, and some others of like mind, including Robespierre and his friends from Arras, had discussed the line they would take in the debates of the Commons. It was now thrown open to any deputy and any respectable citizen who could afford a subscription of 24s. a year, and who wanted to take part in a less formal discussion of the questions before the Assembly. It took its colour from the parliamentary majority of the moment. Here Robespierre soon found himself at home, and his sententious moralisings flourished into real eloquence under the applause of the Parisian *bourgeoisie,* and more particularly its womenfolk. Not for him the rival *Society of Friends of the Rights of Man,* known from its Franciscan premises on the south bank as the Cordeliers Club, where Danton and his extremist friends could be heard for a penny a month denouncing whatever might be the Government of the day to the discontented shopkeepers, students, and artisans of the *Quartier Latin.* Not for him, either, until induced by party urgency, the popular societies where Marat, the "Friend of the People", expounded the Rights of Man to workers whose poverty and shabby clothes excluded them from the Assembly, the clubs, or the cafés.

But no shrewd provincial could remain unaware of the pressure of public opinion on the proceedings of the Assembly; of the competition for seats in the public galleries of the *manège,* and the not infrequent demonstrations of approval or dissent; of the crowds in the cafés or at the street-corners discussing the papers or posters (*affiches*); of the cheers and counter-cheers of partisans at political allusions in the play of the hour; or of the occasional incidents that showed how easily the People, usually so orderly and good-tempered, might become a mob that plundered the house of an unpopular employer or murdered a baker suspected of withholding his stock of bread. Even more ominous were the invisible influences that more and more threatened to distort the vision of Robespierre and those who shared his political ideals: the power of money, in the hands of bankers and speculators; the power of the press, which could be exercised by anyone who could persuade a printer to issue two small pages twice a week; and (in the very heart of the Assembly) the power of party spirit—for it was already the weakness of French politicians to prefer a "pure" minority to a majority based on compromise.

It was a relief to ignore these signs of danger, and to press on with the immediate business of the new Parliament: the drawing up of a constitution, the settling of the relations of Church and State, national finance, and local administration. These matters occupied the Assembly during the first eighteen months of its session; their settlement may be called the constructive work of the Revolution of 1789—however much varied and deformed by subsequent developments; and Robespierre's part in them illustrates the first phase of his political career.

An *assemblée constituante* must enact a constitution. But had not France already got a constitution—a monarchy, one of the oldest in Europe, its origin and successions blessed by the Catholic Church? Yes; and there was no intention of breaking with this tradition. But ever since

Montesquieu had published his comparative study of constitutions, commending the real or imaginary merits of the British method of government, ever since Rousseau had declared that the sovereignty in the State, to whatever form of government power might be delegated, rested in the will of the whole people, and ever since the American rebels, with the help of French arms, had shaken off the control of a monarch not unlike Louis XVI, and were living happily under a republican constitution, Frenchmen had become freshly critical of a Government which legislated and taxed without consulting their wishes, and under which they had no rights corresponding to their duties and no liberties which might not be overruled or taken away. The new constitution was therefore to be a monarchy, but a limited or constitutional one. It would embody, as a preface, the Declaration of Rights: it would give French citizenship and (within certain restrictions) voting power to all Frenchmen of twenty-five and to several classes of foreigners; the executive power would remain in the hands of the King and his ministers, but the legislative power would be transferred to a single-chamber Assembly, unconstrained by any House of Peers or royal veto, or even by a Cabinet; for the ministers, appointed by the King, could not be chosen from amongst the deputies, and were supervised by committees of the House; an army and navy were provided for, but could not be used for police purposes except by the civil authorities, whilst the King could not mobilise them for war purposes without the leave of the Assembly.

Though Robespierre approved in general terms of the Constitution of 1791, and even edited a paper in the following year called *Defénseur de la constitution,* there were many points in it which he disliked. Citizenship had been granted generously, but the right to vote was restricted to those who paid taxes equivalent to three days' wages. This provision, which might seem derisory under modern conditions, at that time excluded from the franchise some two out of six million adult Frenchmen. Robespierre protested against it in the name of the Declaration of Rights, which had asserted that "every citizen has the right to assist personally . . . in the imposition of taxes": sovereignty [he claimed] resides in the people, and is shared by every member of the people; and that involves the right to vote. His protest was ignored by the radical majority, who feared the conservatism of the country-side; indeed, it was never taken to heart till universal male suffrage was at last conceded in 1848. For candidates for the legislature, in which the *bourgeoisie* were determined to keep their majority, a much stiffer qualification was proposed—the payment of taxes equivalent to fifty days' wages. Again Robespierre protested, and in the final revision of the Constitution, two years later, it was allowed that "any active citizen [i.e. anyone having a vote] can be elected to represent the nation"; but at the same time the qualification for electors was stiffened, so as to secure much the same result. Again Jews, actors, Protestants, and domestic servants were generally regarded as unfit to vote; and Robespierre's championship of the first three classes won little support. Domestics were still regarded as part of the hated feudal system. As for women's suffrage, it was not so much as thought of, and remains to this day an un-French idea.

It is to be noticed that the Constitution, so-called "of 1791," was, in fact, enacted bit by bit—here a little and there a little—over a period of more than two years. By way of contrast, the Act called the Civil Constitution of the Clergy was passed at one sitting, in July 1790. This was because it was needed to deal with a concrete and dangerous situation and had behind it the passions as well as the convictions of the deputies. The Catholic Church in France was the most wealthy and powerful corporation in the country. Though its monasteries were half-empty, yet its 150 dioceses and 35,000 benefices, with property in lands, buildings, and endowments estimated at anything between a half and a fifth of the national wealth, constituted a power which, if not conciliated, might wreck the Revolution. The situation was aggravated on the one side by the spiritual dependence of the Church on the Pope, and on the other by the bankruptcy of the State. This second consideration was the starting-point of the whole measure. When, on August 4, the clergy accepted the abolition of the unpopular tithe payments, they expected compensation from the Treasury. When the people decided that they would no longer pay taxes, and when nobody would subscribe to Necker's loans, there was nothing for it but for the State to take over (national-ise, we should say) the property of the Church and to make itself responsible for the payment of the clergy.

In doing this it was natural enough to reorganise the Church as a national institution: to identify the dioceses with the new departments (*départements*), which now replaced the old *généralités* (districts supervised by an *intendant*); to reduce the number of town parishes; to extend to the appointment of parish clergy the democratic method of popular election; to enforce regulations against absenteeism; to standardise the payments both of bishops and clergy; and, as they were now salaried State servants, to demand of them all an oath of allegiance "to the nation, the law, and the King". Some of these provisions were acceptable enough to the parish clergy, whose incomes were thereby improved, and who welcomed reform; even the bishops, whose sometimes huge incomes were reduced to £600–£1,000 a year, would have preferred the Papacy to accept the Constitution rather than to let the French Church fall into schism. But owing to the in-transigence of the Pope, the anti-revolutionary feeling of many of the clergy, the growing impatience of the Assem-bly, and other causes, accommodation proved impossible: Pius VI anathematised the Revolution; many of the bishops (all of whom at this time came from aristocratic families) went into exile; and some 50 per cent. of the clergy refused to take the prescribed oath. The result was that, instead of the Constitutional Church becoming (as it might have been) the nation at prayer, its clergy were a small and increasingly politically-minded minority; whilst the non-juror clergy (or *réfractaires*) were harried by penal laws, and driven out of the country or into hiding.

Although, or maybe just because, he had been brought up in Catholic schools, Robespierre shared the anti-clericalism of most of his fellow-deputies; but his outbreak against the Archbishop of Nîmes had shown that his religion had something more than theirs—a passionate Puritanism that might borrow fuel from Rousseau's *Emile* and use it for the fires of an Inquisition. At present he was content to support the nationalisation of Church property, and the treatment of the clergy as "simply magistrates whose duty it is to maintain and carry on public worship". They should be appointed by popular election and paid like other public officials. He even proposed that they should be allowed to marry—a suggestion which many of them approved, and subsequently acted upon, but which was as yet too novel to be embodied in the settlement. Later, as a result of a visit to Arras at the end of 1791, Robespierre was painfully impressed by the benighted ecclesiasticism of his native town, and returned to Paris a declared enemy of the priesthood. "Every time an aristocratic priest makes a convert [he wrote], he turns him into a fresh enemy of the Revolution." From now onwards he would back the penal legislation against the "refractory" clergy, and would end by putting forward a new creed and a new Church designed to do what the Civil Constitution had failed to do—unite the nation in a simple worship of God freed from Catholic dogma and clerical fanaticism.

The national bankruptcy had necessitated the nationalisation of Church property. It remained to discover the best way to make use of it. It might have been administered by some Ecclesiastical Commission, and anything that could be saved from Church expenses paid into the Treasury. But the immediate demand was for more land and more cash. It was therefore decided to put the property up bit by bit to auction, and to issue through the local authorities certificates exchangeable for a part-ownership of national property (*biens nationaux*). The scheme caught the popular fancy, and within a few years a great part of the lands and buildings formerly belonging to the Church, the crown, or emigrant landlords passed into the hands of the *bourgeoisie* of the towns, the farmers, and even (in small lots) the peasants of the country-side. Two results followed. First, there came into being a new class of land-owners who owed their property to the Revolution, and would support any government that prevented its restoration to the crown, the Church, or the landlords. Secondly, the Government was tempted by the traffic in certificates (*assignats*) to turn them into a paper currency, and by the easiness of multiplying them to issue so many that their value steadily depreciated, till within two years a paper note with face value of 100 *livres* (about £5) was not worth much more than £1. Robespierre was not an economist, and it is not on record that he realised any more than most of his colleagues the dangers of inflation. He was content to attack the hoarders of gold (*accaparateurs*), the speculators in currency (*agioteurs*), and the foreign bankers, who were thought to be manipulating the market in order to weaken and discredit the Government. In any case, he may well have felt that the experiment of the *assignats* was justified; for it saved the Revolution from the bankruptcy of the old regime.

Under the old regime local administration had meant the division of the country into a confused pattern of overlapping civil, judicial, military, and ecclesiastical districts—the *généralités* with their *intendants,* the *bailliages* and *sénéchaussées* with their courts and judges, and the *diocèses* with their bishops and clergy. Behind these divisions lay the old *provinces* of Brittany, Gascony, and the rest, with their differing customs, speech, and loyalties. To an age of reason, and to a national assembly, it seemed intolerable that a country which nature had designed for unity, and a people who were unanimous in their desire for a New Order, should be divided by such antiquated and senseless institutions. If there must be subdivisions, let them be of approximately equal size, and let them be the same for all purposes. So France was freshly divided (by 1794) into 83 *départements,* 556 *districts,* 4,770 *cantons,* and 41,007 *municipalités.* The capital (*chef-lieu*) of the department was also the cathedral city of the diocese and what we should call an Assize town. Each department and district had, for local government, its general Council and permanent Directory, whose members were appointed by popular election. In place of the old centralisation, this plan carried decentralisation almost *ad absurdum;* and Robespierre was one of the first to realise that, if the country was to be governed efficiently, some means must be devised to instruct and discipline the thousands of ignorant and inexperienced men who now controlled or obstructed local administration. When Jacobinism came into power a few years later, its main effort was directed towards *re*-centralisation. But at the moment more was to be gained by enlisting keen young men up and down the country in the cause of the Revolution than by discouraging local enthusiasm; and the hopes that the new system would really unify the provinces seemed to be justified by the great Fête of Federation held in Paris on the first anniversary of the fall of the Bastille, when armed deputations from all over France met on the Champ de Mars to hear Mass and a *Te Deum,* and to take an oath of allegiance to the Nation, the Law, and the Crown: "a really sublime and magnificent spectacle", which is still remembered when, on every July 14, Parisians dance in the streets of their capital.

Chapter 3

From Monarchy to Republic

AT THE END of the first year of revolution, as the winter
of 1790 changed into the spring of 1791, the course of
public affairs, and with it Robespierre's career, seemed
to be slowing down to a rather profitless routine. The
constitution was on paper, but only in part enforced: the
Church settlement had set priest against priest, and deprived half the parishes in the country of confession and
the Mass; prices were going up and values down; the
country labourer complained that feudalism was not really
abolished, and the town workman that under the new
regime (culminating in the *loi le Chapelier,* June 14,
1791) he was not allowed to agitate for better wages,
whilst any political demonstration might be met by a
declaration of martial law and the muskets of the National
Guard. The new legislation embodying the "ideas of '89"
was being sabotaged, sometimes by the King's ministers,
sometimes by the ill will of counter-revolutionary members
of departmental committees, sometimes by the stupidity
or local prejudices of mayors and town councillors, who
might well be excused by the number and complexity of
the decrees showered upon them by the Paris post. Almost
everywhere enthusiasm was giving way to disillusionment,
and the fraternity of equal citizens to the fears and hatreds
of rival parties and competing programmes.

Robespierre himself, overworked by attendance seven
days a week at the Assembly and at the Jacobin Club,
by speech-making, letter-writing (though he was a bad
correspondent), a judicial appointment at Versailles, and
other duties, was also troubled by misrepresentations in
the press and attacks by his constituents at Arras. With
all his ambition, he had a thin skin; and a small man's
touchiness and suspicion. He took offence, and gave it.
He was feared more than admired, and admired more than

liked. Probably this did not trouble him, so long as he could pursue a consistent course, and make himself necessary to the party which he believed would some day come into power. No one in the Assembly was so consistently the spokesman of the lost cause, as it now might seem, of Liberty and Equality, no one so continuously the champion of popular rights, no one so definitely in opposition to the *bourgeois* monopoly of power.

The Revolution might seem to be at a standstill; but, in fact, it was moving rapidly towards its greatest crisis— the fall of the throne. How did this come about? Ever since October 6, 1789, when Louis had consented to move from Versailles to Paris, his crown had been in danger; it might soon be his life. This was the text of Mirabeau's warnings, and the ground of the advice which he submitted in a series of Notes through his friend the Comte de la Marck between June 1790 and February 1791. A native of the Midi, Mirabeau had a southerner's distrust of the capital, which absorbed so much of the food and wealth and talent of the country. An aristocrat, he felt ill at ease amongst his *bourgeois* fellow-deputies (fighting, too, at every turn against his bad reputation), and distrusted their irresponsible meddling with the science and art of government. His monarchism was not, like theirs, a sentiment, but a conviction. He knew that France needed a strong Executive, and that it must rest in the hands of the King and his ministers, though supervised by the Legislature and responsible to the people. But he was neither consistent nor fastidious in the means he proposed to secure this end. At one time he was working for the choice of certain deputies—meaning primarily himself—as ministers; at another time for active cooperation between himself and Necker, or Lafayette; and when both schemes failed, for the creation of a King's party in the country, to command a majority in a new Assembly; but always at the back of his mind was the feeling that Louis must leave Paris, and appeal to the royalist provinces—from Rouen, preferably—against the growing republicanism of the capital.

But Louis and Marie-Antoinette, though they paid him for his advice, would not take it. They only trusted their old friends—the few who still remained with them: la Marck; Mercy d'Argenteau (the Austrian ambassador); de Bouillé, in command of troops on the eastern frontier; and Fersen, an officer in the Swedish Guard, a personal friend of the Queen. This group had for months been working out a plan for an escape, not to Rouen but to the Rhine; to be followed by an appeal, not to royalist Frenchmen but to the Austrian army, and the exiled (*émigrés*) nobles who were drilling beyond the frontier and praying for vengeance on the Parisians. When in April 1791 the King's Catholic scruples prevented his conforming to the Civil Constitution which he had unwillingly sanctioned, and he would have gone to Saint-Cloud to receive his Easter communion from a nonjuror priest, a crowd, half suspecting an attempt to escape, prevented his journey. This proof that he was, in fact, a prisoner finally determined Louis to carry out his wife's plan. On the night of June 20 the royal family, disguised and carrying false passports, escaped from the Tuileries, and drove away on the road for Châlons and Montmédy, where they hoped to pause, within sight of the Austrian army, before making the irremediable move across the frontier. But they were recognised on their way, and at Varennes, only a few miles short of their goal, they were stopped, arrested, and ignominiously brought back to Paris. No excuses could explain away such an act of disloyalty to the country and the throne. It changed the whole course of the Revolution.

The Assembly behaved with unexpected coolness in the crisis caused by the flight to Varennes, and France quickly learnt how to do without a king. But it soon became clear that Paris and the Assembly were at issue about the King's treatment and the future government of the country. The constitution was waiting for his signature; and that would mean, for the deputies, the crowning of their two years' work and an opportunity for honourable retirement. He must therefore be reinstated; if he were not, the constitution would fall to the ground, and all their work would have to be done over again. But Paris was bitterly indignant against the King and Queen, whose flight had justified all their suspicions. The Cordeliers Club, the more radical members of the Jacobins, and the Popular Societies talked openly of dethroning the King and setting up a Republic. Robespierre, without going so far as republicanism, held that Louis should be brought to trial, like any other recaptured *émigré,* and he found himself voting with a small minority in the House against the temporary "suspension" (as opposed to permanent "deposition") of the King, to be followed by his reinstatement, so soon as he had signed the Constitution. He even agreed to the Jacobins joining the Cordeliers in a public petition for deposition. But when the Assembly, on July 16, decreed suspension, such action became illegal, and his professional caution made the Jacobins withdraw from the petition which the Cordeliers put out for public signature on the 17th, calling for the King's trial and the setting up of "a new Executive Power". The word "republic" was not used, but martial law was proclaimed by the Assembly, and the demonstrators were dispersed by the National Guard, under the orders of Bailly (the mayor of Paris) and Lafayette, suffering some fifty casualties. The "Massacre of the Champ de Mars" was followed by a prescription of popular leaders and papers. Robespierre, owing to his last-minute withdrawal, escaped; but the more conservative members of the Jacobins seceded, and it was some weeks before the club recovered its popularity.

During the crisis, partly for safety, partly for convenience, Robespierre left his lodgings in the *Marais,* and took a room at 366, rue Saint-Honoré, within easy reach of the Club and the Assembly. He was now more assiduous than ever in his attendance at both. In the Assembly he found himself more than ever the spokesman of the Opposition, defending the rights of the common man against attempts, inspired by the new fear of republicanism, to stiffen the conditions of franchise before the constitution took its final form. It was now that he proposed the "Self-denying Ordinance" by which no member of the Constituent Assembly would be eligible for the Legislative Assembly due to take its place under the new constitution. The proposal, perhaps to his own surprise, was carried; for most of the deputies thought they had done their work in Paris, and wished to return home after two and a half years' exile. The most serious result of this measure was, of course, that the new Assembly would be deprived of the experience gained in the old; and historians have generally lamented this. But Robespierre intended it; for he held that the old deputies had grown out of touch with public opinion, which was moving towards republicanism; and he held that there were as good men in the country as ever came out of it—men who had already forgotten the old regime and would not obstruct the march of the new. Certainly it was significant that, when on September 30 the King had signed the constitution and the Assembly was dissolved, Robespierre and his supporter, Pétion, were chaired by the crowd, amidst cries of *Vive la Liberté!—Vive Robespierre!— Vive l'Incorruptible!*—the proud title which he had earned by refusal of every inducement to abandon the popular cause.

Robespierre's change of lodgings in the summer of 1791 brought a change in his way of life. Instead of the quiet of the rue Saintonge where he had one fellow-lodger, he was now a member of a large family circle in one of the busiest streets of the city. His host, Maurice Duplay, was a prosperous carpenter and builder, with a politically-minded wife, a boy still at school, an orphaned nephew, and three marriageable daughters. In the eldest of these, the plain earnest Eléonore, Robespierre found a soul-mate, and in the whole household an audience of admirers. "He was the best brother a girl could have," said her younger sister Elisabeth, "a model of virtue, and we all loved him dearly." They gave him an upstairs bed-sitting-room, where he had his desk, his book-shelves, and the constant accumulation of political papers and pamphlets.

Here he spent all the time he could spare from the Club and the Assembly, writing his speeches and planning the future of his party and of his career. In the evenings Mme Duplay would keep open house for their political friends and neighbours: Pétion, afterwards Mayor of Paris; Fouché, the ex-monk, later terrorist and Bonaparte's chief of Police; Desmoulins, who perished three years later with the Dantonists; Le Bas, Elisabeth's fiancé; Saint-Just, whom admiration for Robespierre had turned into a Jacobin; David the painter; Couthon the crippled fanatic; Nicolas the Government printer, and many others. Sometimes they would have music, when Le Bas sang Italian opera; sometimes Robespierre would recite his favourite speeches from Corneille or Racine. Or there would be an evening at the *Théâtre Français,* or a country excursion, when Robespierre would take with him his sketch-book and a bag of oranges, and his dog "Brount". But these were only occasional diversions from the daily round of Assembly from 10 to 3 or 4, and of Club from 6 to 8 or 10, without any of the recesses or week-ends that make modern parliamentary life bearable. And though Robespierre's social interests and human sympathies were evidently expanding in this new atmosphere, there was no relaxation of his political singleness of mind. If anything, under the stress of party controversy and national danger, he was himself becoming more controversial, more fanatical, more dangerous.

That he now thought of Paris and the rue Saint-Honoré as his real home can be read between the lines of his visit to Arras, as soon as the Assembly dissolved, in October 1791. His journey there was almost a triumphal procession, and he found the town illuminated in his honour. But the municipality stood aloof, and he had enemies amongst the clergy and aristocrats. From the letters he wrote to Duplay at this time, it is clear that Arras opened his eyes to the danger of counter-revolutionary intrigues in the frontier provinces and of royalist activities on the part of the non-juror clergy. The results of his experiences were soon seen in his speeches and policy; for both matters were becoming of urgent importance in the months following the flight to Varennes.

The King's plan of escape had been known to the Emperor Leopold; he had, indeed, made his help conditional on its success. What would be his attitude, now that it had failed and that his brother-in-law had been restored to a diminished throne, the trustee of a constitution he did not believe in, and the prisoner of a city and Government rapidly moving towards republicanism? Ever since 1756 Austria had been a nominal ally of France. The marriage of the present Emperor's sister to the heir of the French throne had been a renewal of that alliance and a gesture of solidarity between the only Catholic sovereigns north of the Alps. But it was a dynastic alliance, never popular amongst Frenchmen, and much less so since the Revolution, the emigration of officers and aristocrats over the German frontier, and now the incident of Varennes. Paris was no farther from the Rhine, in the fears of its citizens, than London from the Straits of Dover. Secret agents were passing to and fro, and rumour did not lessen their numbers. The royal princes, the King's brothers, had refused his appeal to return to the country, and were urging Leopold to take military action. The royal princesses, the King's aunts, had successfully emigrated to Rome. But Leopold was a more cautious man than his predecessor Joseph, and less interested in the fate of his unfortunate sister. He distrusted the warlike attitude of his Prussian ally, Frederick William, rightly supposing that he was more anxious to acquire French territory than to champion the Bourbon monarchy. He consented to the Declaration of Pillnitz (August 27, 1791) threatening their joint armed intervention, but hoped not to have to implement it.

The decision was taken out of his hands by the action of the French Government. The Legislative Assembly, which met on October 1, was composed of new men—not younger than their predecessors or noticeably more radical, but without their hard-won experience of public affairs or of the Parisian point of view. They were there

to enforce a constitution in which no one much believed—
only the King, it was said, had studied how to use it
against the Assembly; and their debates were conducted
under the critical eyes of ex-deputies and the double
threat of republicanism and war. It was little wonder that
they were hurried into rash courses by an active clique of
ambitious and eloquent members—Brissot, Vergniaud,
Guadet, Gensonné, and their political hostess, Mme Roland—who were the founders of what in the next Assembly came to be called the Girondin party. These men
were not republicans, but their policy played into the
hands of republicanism: for they preached war, and they
hoped that war would put them into power, with the army
in their hands and the King under their feet. But they
were talkers, men of theory (*idéologues* was Bonaparte's
word for them), not statesmen or men of action. They
failed to reckon the real dangers of the situation either
at home or abroad.

Robespierre, Pétion, and those who had voted with
them in the old Assembly were now out of political life,
and could not hope for much support in the new House.
But Pétion was elected Mayor of Paris—an omen which
Brissot might have noted—and Robespierre became editor
of a paper which he called *Le Défenseur de la Constitution*—not that he believed in the Constitution of 1791,
but because he was afraid of premature attempts to revise
it in the interests of Brissot's party. He did not profess
republicanism, but he would prefer it to a puppet monarchy in the hands of a reactionary *bourgeoisie*. At all costs
he was opposed to war. He believed the army was in no
state to fight; he knew that the country was riddled with
counter-revolutionary intrigue; and he foresaw that the
nation in arms would become an easy prey for the first
successful general who had the ability and ambition to
seize power. In a series of articles and speeches he worked
up feeling against Brissot and his war policy—isolating
himself from most of his friends, and risking his popularity with the common people—his "incorruptibility" was
never put to so severe a test. And it all seemed in vain;

for when on March 1 Leopold died, and was succeeded by the incautious Francis, and when, ten days later, Louis accepted a ministry nominated by Brissot, the new Foreign Minister, Dumouriez, hurried him into an ultimatum, and hostilities became inevitable: On April 20 Louis, with the approval of the Assembly, declared war against the King of Hungary and Bohemia, and France began an adventure which only ended on the field of Waterloo.

Within a week Robespierre's judgment of the situation was justified. In the first clash with the Austrians on the Belgian frontier, the French troops ran away and murdered one of their generals. The Minister of War and the Commander-in-Chief resigned. Whilst the King thought only how he could use the defeat to rid himself of the Brissotins, Brissot thought only how he could use it to discredit and disarm the King. On May 30 Louis was deprived of his palace troops and left to the dubious protection of sentinels from the National Guard; a few days later it was determined to establish a camp for provincial troops on the way to the front close outside Paris—a threat both to the King and to the political Opposition. Louis retaliated on June 13 by dismissing his *Brissotin* ministry and falling back on the few royalists who were ready to risk a last throw. He was prepared for whatever might befall: at best, an advance of Austrian troops on Paris, making rescue or escape possible; at worst, the defence of the Tuileries against attack by armed citizens and *fédérés* (national volunteers from the provinces), who regarded the royal palace as a centre of counter-revolution, an outpost of the Austrian invader.

One June 20 the democratic quarters of the city organised a demonstration to plant a "tree of liberty" on the north terrace of the Tuileries gardens and to present petitions to the King and the Assembly. The crowd soon got out of hand, invaded the gardens, forced an entrance into the place, and for two hours compelled the royal family to listen to speeches and insults. Louis' impassivity passed for courage: he put on a red cap of liberty, and drank to the health of the nation; but insisted that he would stand by his rights under the Constitution. No such gesture could now save a lost cause. A young Corsican officer named Bonaparte, who watched the scene in the gardens, remarked that if he were king he would not tolerate such things—and he lived to apply the lesson. Another soldier, Lafayette, was so horrified that he left his command at the front to protest against the faction which had incited the crowd, to appeal to the loyalty of the National Guard, and to offer means of escape to the King. He failed, and within six weeks threw up his command, only to be interned in an Austrian prison.

The public temper was such that nothing now could save the crown; but it needed new leaders. Brissot and his party were being outvoted in the House, and outbidden in the streets by Robespierre, Danton, and the leaders of the democratic quarters of the city. They began to fear that when the crown fell, it would not be into the hands of their party, but into those of the Paris Commune—the enemies of the provincial *bourgeoisie,* and of any puppet-king—the out-and-out republicans. They even made last-minute attempts to save the throne; whilst the Jacobins organised revolutionary committees to direct a fresh and final attack upon the Tuileries.

On July 14 the anniversary of the Fall of the Bastille was once more celebrated on the Champ de Mars. Louis was there, but he wore a breast-plate under his robes of state, and the cheers of the crowd went to Pétion, whom he had tried to depose from the mayoralty for allowing the disorders of June 20, and who was already deliberating how best to shut his eyes to the next invasion of the Tuileries. On July 30 the forces of insurrection were strengthened by the arrival in Paris of 500 *fédérés* from Marseille, singing the war-song of the army of the Rhine, the *Marseillaise.* These men fraternised with the Jacobins, and were persuaded to postpone their march to the front till they had dealt with the "Austrian Committee" at the Tuileries. This was the name now given to the Queen and her advisers, who were more than suspected of treasonable correspondence with the enemy, and who inspired a declaration issued in the last days of July by the Duke of Brunswick, the Prussian general, threatening to punish any attack upon the Tuileries "by delivering up Paris to military execution and complete destruction".

The result was what might have been expected. On August 3 every quarter of the city but one joined in a petition for the deposition of the King and the summoning of a National Convention. On the night of August 9–10 the rising, which had been twice postponed, broke out with irresistible force. An Insurrectionary Commune occupied the Town Hall, suspended the legally elected municipal authorities, and directed the armed National Guards and *fédérés* to march on the Tuileries. The palace should have been amply defended by some veteran *Suisses* and aristocrat volunteers whom Louis had brought in, as well as by 2,000 "royalist" National Guardsmen called out by the Paris Department to safeguard the Executive Power, as the King was now called. But Mandat, their commandant, obeyed a summons to the Town Hall, where he was murdered, and his command transferred to a popular Jacobin, Santerre; Pétion, the mayor, soon made an excuse for leaving the palace; and when Mandat's men greeted Louis with cries of *Vive la nation!* and *A bas le véto!* he was persuaded by Roederer, the clerk (*procureur*) of the Paris Department, to evacuate the palace, and to put himself and his family under the protection of the Assembly in the neighbouring *manège*. There they sat all day, whilst the people stormed and looted the palace and massacred the *Suisses,* whom Louis had belatedly told to lay down their arms.

Such were the circumstances in which "the French people [as the commemorative medal put it] won a glorious combat against tyranny at the Tuileries". So the Revolution passed from Monarchy to Republicanism.

Chapter 4

Commune and Convention

THE EVENTS OF August 10, 1792, puzzled as well as horrified foreign observers. Englishmen, who remembered the way in which George III and John Wilkes had dealt with the Gordon Riots only twelve years before, could not understand an attack on the King of France in his royal palace led by the city police and condoned by the Lord Mayor. It still needs explanation. What we have hitherto called the "quarters" of Paris were in fact the forty-eight *sections* into which the city had been divided under the municipal law of 1790. Previously sixty electoral *districts* or city constituencies, they were now regrouped, with the intention of weakening their independent attitude towards the City Council (*municipalité* or *commune*). But, in fact, each *section,* whose population averaged 12,500 and whose "active citizens" (voters), averaging 1,700, provided at once the nucleus of a political club and of a battalion of the National Guard, became more than ever a political unit, controlled by whatever party had the majority in its counsels, and able to back its demands by force of arms. Some of these *sections*—those of the more fashionable quarters—still held by the King; others, notably the crowded quarters of the east end and south bank, were violently republican. Many wavered between the two opinions. When the outbreak of war was followed by four months of defeat and the invasion of the country, all but one were for the deposition of the King; but it was only after much pressure, haranguing, and intriguing that a sufficient majority was secured to carry through the insurrection of August 10. So strong still was the instinct for central direction that it was necessary to dispossess the *municipalité,* the formally elected representatives of the *sections,* and to carry out the revolt in the name of an "Insurrectionary Commune". It was paradoxical that the Paris *département,* of which the city was only a part, should be obliged to defend the King against the people and police of Paris; but the municipality had long been in the habit of brushing aside the reactionary departmental directory, and the Insurrectionary Commune had no scruples in doing so again.

August 10 left the Insurrectionary Commune in command of the field. True, the Assembly was still sitting—but a mere Rump: the ministers still attended their offices—but without an Executive Power to give them status; the Constitution was still in force—but without the monarchy which was essential to it; the armies still stood on the frontiers—but would their generals transfer their allegiance to a republic? France as a whole still held to the Revolution and could do without a king; but was it prepared to tolerate a dictatorship of the Paris Commune? These issues distracted the country for the six weeks between the fall of the throne (August 10) and the meeting of the National Convention (September 20). They were immensely aggravated by the news that the Duke of Brunswick had crossed the frontier and that a Prussian army was marching on Paris.

The events of these six weeks may be looked at through the eyes of Robespierre. In the middle of May, when he published the first number of his *Défenseur de la Constitution,* his condemnation of the war had been justified by defeats at the front, and his championship of the constitution by the evident intention of Brissot's party to overthrow it in their own interests. But he had no constructive ideas about the war—only the peevish criticisms of a passivist; and he was not ready to support openly the republicanism which he secretly believed to be inevitable until he could be sure of the success of the impending insurrection. He was a man of principle, an Incorruptible; but he was also an ambitious man, a careerist of an unusual kind—ambitious not for power to rule but for influence to lead; not for the rôle of a dictator but of a prophet, perhaps of a martyr.

Yes; but in what cause? The answer can be put in his

own words. "The issue of the Revolution is quite simple. . . . If the old abuses persist under new names, if the new forms of government are no better than the old . . . what do I care whether we have a dictator or a king, a parliament or a senate, tribunes or consuls? . . . The sole aim of society being the preservation of the imprescriptible rights of man, the only proper motive of a revolution should be to recover these rights from the usurption of tyranny and force." But that was not all. The rights of man he identifies with "those principles of justice and morality which lie at the root of human society", written in the soul of man, and to be read there by "him who has a pure heart and a virtuous character". He idealises the ideas of 1789, and turns a social revolution into a moral reformation: a transvaluation of values essential to civilisation in the long run, but hopelessly puzzling at the moment to politicians who thought the State could be saved by laws and institutions, or to business-men and workers to whom the New Order meant more profits and higher wages. One more step. To Robespierre the hope of this moral reformation lay in "the People"—that part of the nation least corrupted (as Rousseau would say) by society, best able to break its chains, most representative of the General Will—that Third Estate which had made the Revolution possible and should inherit its blessings.

Thus it was that Robespierre watched the events of the summer of 1792 without actively committing himself to the Jacobin any more than to the Girondin attack on the throne. But he secretly hoped that it would end in the victory of the People, and open a new way to the Republic of Justice and Virtue which was his only ideal. He was not a member of either the federal or the sectional committees which organised the attack of August 10; but he knew what was going on. The chosen representative of the interests of Marseille in the Assembly, he approved the march of their *fédérés* and publicised their part in the insurrection. As August 10 grew near, the *Défenseur* came out openly on the side of the insurrection, and said that it must aim at setting up, in place of both King and Assembly, a truly representative National Convention. But Robespierre did not appear in the streets on August 10, as Desmoulins did, with his sword at his side, nor at the Town Hall, where Danton sat with the Insurrectionary Commune. He stayed at home —his enemies said in the cellar—till it was all over; and in the evening he appeared as usual at the Jacobin Club, with a speech insisting on the election of a Convention, suggesting that official accounts of the day should be circulated throughout the provinces, and advising the People not to disarm until they had secured their liberties. His part in the events of the day was not forgotten; for a medal was struck showing Robespierre drinking a cup held in the hand of Liberty, with the inscription *Régénération française, 10, août, 1792*.

But now he must accommodate his moralism and his ideals to the practical demands of the Insurrectionary Commune, which August 10 had put into power. Was this the People? Could these violent and quarrelsome leaders of the democratic *sections* be shepherded into the true fold; or would his scruples have to give way before the logic of revolution? On August 11 he was elected a member of the Commune, and for a fortnight he attended its meetings. On the 12th, and again on the 22nd, he petitioned the Assembly, in its name, to abolish its rival, the Paris Department. On the 14th he proposed that a monument should be raised in the Place Vendôme, where Louis' statue had recently stood, in honour of the citizen victims of August 10. Next day he demanded that a special court should be set up to judge the surviving *Suisses* —a foretaste of the Revolutionary Tribunal; but when it was instituted he refused to be one of its judges: he still shrank from condemning anyone to death. When the Rump of the Girondist Assembly, on August 25, boldly proposed to dissolve the Insurrectionary Commune and to restore the old *municipalité,* Robespierre backed their refusal to disperse but dissuaded them from violence. In all this it is difficult not to think that his idealism was dragging its anchors in the tide of Parisian resentment.

His excuse was that he was looking forward to the election of a National Convention which should put the Commune in its place and set the Revolution finally on the right lines.

The elections began on August 26, and lasted till September 8. The dates are important, for this fortnight coincided with events which gave an irrevocable turn to the Revolution. The "victory" of August 10 was only five days' old when news came that the Prussian invaders were across the frontier. Within ten days Thionville was invested and Longwy had surrendered. On September 2 it was heard that Verdun, the key fortress on the road to Paris, had also fallen. The enemy was within 140 miles of the capital. This was Danton's moment, not Robespierre's. Whilst the one rigged the elections, the other called on Parisians to march to the defence of their country. "For victory [he cried] we must dare and dare and dare again; and France will be saved." There was a third leader at work. Marat—once a fashionable doctor with a Scottish degree, now a disgruntled "Friend of the People", content to share the slum life of the south bank and to tell the readers of his paper home-truths about the Revolution—now incited a movement for purging the prisons and destroying counter-revolutionaries who, in the absence of any garrison and with the approach of the enemy, might break loose and massacre the patriots. For prisons were by no means the safe places they are now, and their inmates might overpower their few guards and force the doors.

So began the September massacre, in which, during six days, between 1,100 and 1,300 prisoners—priests, aristocrats, prostitutes, and common criminals—were killed by gangs of murderers who went round from one prison to another, with the connivance of the Commune and without any effective intervention by the Assembly. Danton, the Minister of Justice, approved. Roland, the respectable Minister of the Interior, excused it as "a kind of justice". Even Robespierre had by now sunk so low in party spirit that he was credited with having tried to get Roland, Brissot, and other prominent Girondins put in prison, so that they might share the fate of the victims. Certainly he knew what was going on; as certainly he did nothing to stop it. The prison massacre branded a mark of Cain on the forehead of the Jacobin party, and committed Robespierre to a theory of "popular justice" which makes more understandable, if not more excusable, his share in the Terror of 1793–4.

Meanwhile the elections that were being held all over the country, whilst they showed no regret for the monarchy, proved an almost unanimous desire for a new constitution, and that a republican one. True, it was a small poll—not more than a fifth of the electors took the trouble to vote; but that might be put down to the recent surfeit of local elections and to the complications of the method employed. The 750 new deputies, who were to make history, included many members of the two previous Assemblies and many who had held office under the Revolution: predominantly "lawyers", but others drawn from the professions, the arts, and the services; even a handful of repentant aristocrats, and the King's cousin, the Duc d'Orléans. The international outlook of the Revolution was symbolised by the presence amongst the deputies of Tom Paine—one of six Englishmen to whom the Legislative Assembly had accorded honorary French citizenship.

The National Convention had two duties: to defeat the invader and to draft a constitution. By a coincidence which was happy for the Girondins but perhaps not so fortunate for the Assembly, the day of its first session (September 20) was also that of the victory of Valmy, which led to the retreat of the Prussian army across the frontier. Disengaged for the moment from the danger of invasion, the deputies could settle down to an occupation really far more dangerous to the country—that of political recrimination. Every parliament is by derivation a "Talking-house", and Frenchmen were always good talkers. Some limits can be set to irresponsible talking if members of parliament are divided into a Government and an Opposition (whether composed of single parties or of many), one of which is in charge of the policy of the country, whilst the other, if successful in its criticisms, may at any moment become so.

But in the Convention, as in the previous two Assemblies, no such arrangement held. Every prominent deputy was the potential centre of a party, or rather clique. The Government was in the hands of the majority of the moment, which tried to maintain its position by electing a fortnightly President and Secretaries from its own set, and by securing a majority on the Standing Committees of the House which supervised the ministers. Since no by-elections were held (substitutes called *suppléants* having been nominated beforehand) and no one could dissolve parliament, the "opinion of the country" could not be consulted; and since there was no Cabinet to resign and no Opposition bench to takes its place, a "party majority" might fluctuate endlessly, until some decisive vote forced an issue, or (as was likely enough in the long run) the Sovereign People, disguised as the Paris *sections,* intervened, and purged the Assembly of deputies it no longer held to be its true representatives.

In such a House of Commons the long views of statemanship went by default, and the short views of partisanship too often prevailed. Personal abuse, unrestrained by any law of libel, occasionally led to a duel; but anyone who reads the minutes (*procès-verbaux*) of the debates will agree with the view of contemporary Parisians that "scenes in the House" were a welcome relief in the dreary round of solemn committee reports and long-winded written speeches which made up the bulk of the proceedings. No deputy to the Convention had been elected on a "party ticket", though much had been done, particularly in Paris, to exclude from the polls persons suspected of royalism or counter-revolution. The Jacobins and Girondins, as they might now be fairly called, were not definite parties, but groups of like-minded individuals. Their leaders were never a Cabinet: for no deputy could be a minister. Their prestige rested on their personalities, their oratorical gifts, their connection with some powerful club, or *section,* or paper. It would be almost a miracle if in such an Assembly a definite pattern of policy emerged and established itself.

Nevertheless, the contest between Jacobin and Girondin was a real struggle between rival views of political methods and rival ways of revolutionary life. All 750 deputies were pledged to national defence and to a republican constitution. Most of them remained faithful to these two aims, and voted for whatever proposals seemed most likely to secure them: these were the *marais,* the "Bloomsbury set", the moderate and respectable majority of the Assembly, who gave some continuity to its policy and saved it in the long run from the aberrations of its extremist members. At either end of this moderate majority were two minorities—one large, one small; and these, consisting of men who had definite views and agreed policies provided the equivalent of a "Government" and an "Opposition", carrying with them varying proportions of the moderate votes of the centre. The majority, on the Right, were called Girondins, because their best speakers were deputies from the Gironde department. The minority, on the Left, were called Jacobins, because their leaders were Paris deputies, prominent members of the Jacobin Club. But it would be useless to try to show that the rank and file of the Jacobins came from one part of France and the Girondins from another; or that they belonged to different classes of society. All that can be said is that the Girondins on the whole represented the "men of '89", who thought that the aims of the Revolution could be procured by good laws, an appeal to reason, and economic *laissez-faire;* whilst the Jacobins on the whole represented the more experienced and disillusioned view of 1791–2, and believed in the need for a greater measure of central control. So far, the Girondins might be called idealists and the Jacobins realists. Looking further ahead, the Girondins wanted a state in which middle-class profits and investments would be secure and life enjoyable: the Jacobin Utopia was to be a planned democracy, a Welfare Dictatorship.

Robespierre's own view can be read in the articles which he now published in his new journal; it was a continuation of the *Défenseur,* but with a grey instead of a red cover, and renamed after Mirabeau's periodical of 1789, *Lettres de Maximilien Robespierre à ses commettans* ("Letters to his constituents"). He is still more of a reformer than a revolutionist. The business of the Convention, he thinks, is "to perfect the organisation and distribution of the constituted authorities . . . to dilute aristocracy with new institutions . . . and to guarantee sovereign rights". In other words, he wants, at the moment, no more than a republican revision of the Constitution of 1791; he will not trust the Girondin majority an inch further. But obviously there is much more behind, which only the triumph of the Jacobin party can secure.

"It is not enough to have overturned the throne: our concern is to erect upon its remains holy equality, and the imprescriptible rights of man. It is not an empty name, but the character of its citizens, that constitutes a republic. The soul of a republic is *vertu*—that is, love of one's country, and a high-minded devotion which sinks all private interests in those of the community as a whole."

The real problem before the legislator is to govern without oppression; the ideal constitution would provide control without the risk of abuse or corruption—"The temple of liberty must be rebuilt upon the foundations of justice and equality."

Such sentiments might sound as vague as those of political idealists commonly do; but when they were reinforced by Robespierre's will and by the ambitions of a political minority, backed by the popular feeling of a great capital, they became potent and dangerous.

Chapter 5

The Fate of the Girondins

THE END OF September 1792, when the enemy had barely turned back from Paris, the prison massacres were not three weeks old, and the royal family was interned in the Temple under the charge of the Commune, was no time for visionary Utopias. Victory had to be confirmed and completed. The National Convention had to settle accounts with the Parisian Commune. The fate of the King had to be determined. A constitution had to be drawn up. From the first the Girondin majority, controlling the presidency (not of an impartial Speaker, but of a temporary chairman entitled to do what he could for his party) and packing the Committees of the House, encouraged the *Brissotin* ministers who had been reappointed on August 10–12 in their polemic against the usurping Commune; particularly the pedantic Roland and his ambitious and spiteful wife, who never tired of finding fault with the conduct of the city authorities, and showed their distrust of the National Guard by summoning 16,000 provincial *fédérés* to the capital to defend the Convention against the people. Not only so; the Girondin leaders missed no opportunity of attacking their rivals—antagonising Robespierre, refusing to work with Danton (whom they replaced at the Ministry of Justice by Garat, a friend of Roland), and bringing Marat to trial. The indictment of Robespierre by the Rolandist J. B. Louvet on October 29 made him responsible for the prison massacre and for the other crimes of the Commune, and accused him of aiming at a dictatorship. His reply a few days later was overwhelming, and he became more than ever the idol of the Jacobin Club and the prophet of the people. The rejection of Danton added a demagogue to the Jacobin ranks: the hero of the national defence and a man whose impressive ugliness (like that of Mirabeau), vulgar democratic manners, and powers of extempore eloquence made him the perfect foil to Robespierre. Marat was no asset to any political party; but it was dangerous to attack the "Friend of the people", and his murder made him the most popular martyr of the Revolution.

Over all these personal quarrels of the two parties hung the inescapable question—what to do with the King? He had been "claimed" from the protection of the Assembly by the victorious Commune, and imprisoned with his family—the Queen, the Dauphin, Madame Royale, and Louis' sister, Princess Elisabeth—in the old tower of the Temple, from which escape was impossible. But though the monarchy had been abolished on September 21, once a king was always a king; and though many royalist nobles had disowned him since he accepted the Constitution, and had transferred their loyalty to his brother, the Comte de Provence, yet Louis Capet, as people now called him, was still a centre of monarchical sentiment in France and of monarchical intrigue abroad; a source of counter-revolutionary infection, expensive to keep in isolation and dangerous to set free. It would have been better if he had been allowed to escape at Varennes; his Austrian relations would have found less reason for restoring him to the throne than for rescuing him from captivity. After his return, there had been a popular clamour for his trial as a traitor. The Assembly had resisted it, and reinstated him—on probation—as a constitutional King. He had again betrayed the Constitution, and the country too, first (it was said) by intriguing with the enemy, and then by shooting down innocent citizens in the defence of the Tuileries. The Girondins had already been accused of royalism when they suspended Louis instead of deposing him after Varennes, and when they tried to defend him from the Commune on August 10. They dared not do more. The Jacobins were clamouring for the King's trial, which they hoped to turn to the discredit of the Girondins, the defeat of royalism and defiance of the monarchs of Europe.

The proposal to try the King raised constitutional questions of some complexity. Was the Convention a competent court? Could Louis be indicted for crimes committed whilst he was on the throne and was covered by the "inviolability" formula in the Constitution; or for crimes committed after his "abdication" at the time of the flight to Varennes, seeing that the clause under which this constituted abdication had been added afterwards; or, again, for crimes committed after the forced deposition of August 10—and, anyhow, what were they? This formidable knot of difficulties Robespierre would cut through by insisting that there was no need to try Louis, but simply to convict and punish him; and the penalty for insurrection against the State was death.

His two speeches on the King's trial (December 3 and 28) are amongst his most eloquent—the more so since they deal with a practical issue, nothing Utopian. "This is no question of a trial," he said on December 3, "Louis is not a defendant; you are not judges, but statesmen, and the representatives of the people. You have not to give a verdict for or against an individual, but to adopt a measure of public safety, and to safeguard the future of the nation. . . ." Louis cannot be tried [he maintained], for he has already been tried and convicted by the institution of the Republic. . . . There is no constitution, no law, no pact to which he can appeal. The insurrection of August 10 leaves nothing standing but the law of nature, and the safety of the people. "We talk of a republic, and Louis still lives! We talk of a republic, and the person of the King still stands between us and liberty!" He went on to admit that he had hitherto been against the death penalty; but there was no alternative: "because the country must live, Louis must die." He reiterated this argument on December 28, dealing with the suggestion of an appeal from the Assembly to the people. The people has already expressed its opinion by dethroning the King: it is for the people's representatives to finish its work by executing the royal traitor.

The Girondin proposal of a *plébiscite* would be rejected. But a semblance of a Westminster trial (many deputies were fully aware of the precedent) was provided by the questioning of the King before the Assembly on December 11, the speech of his Counsel de Sèze, on the 26th, and the solemn casting of votes by the 750 "judges" which began on January 14. Three questions were put: Was Louis guilty? Should the case be referred to the country by a *plébiscite*? What penalty should be inflicted? In the first division 683 out of 748 deputies voted that Louis was guilty; it was a national verdict. In the second —an issue between the Girondins, who counted on the inherent royalism of the country-side, and the Jacobins, who held that the deputies must not shelve their responsibility —286 voted for a *plébiscite,* 425 against: a Jacobin success. On the third and final issue, now unavoidable, the voting went on for twenty-four hours, each deputy speaking in turn, and sometimes giving reasons for his vote. When the votes were at last counted, it was reckoned that 361 had been cast for death *sans phrase* (as one put it), i.e. summary execution, and 72 more for temporary reprieve (*sursis*); 288 deputies had voted for imprisonment or exile. When an additional vote had been taken on the question of reprieve and showed a substantial majority against it, the sense of the House was deemed to be sufficiently clear.

The sentence was carried out early on the morning of January 21, 1793. For two hundred years past, when a Bourbon king died, the cry had been *Le Roi est mort: vive le Roi!* But now, when the crowd saw their King's head fall in the place de la Révolution, they shouted *Vive la nation!* Yet many must have asked the question— could France live without a king?

The predominance of the Girondin party in the Convention was seriously shaken by their failure to save the King's life; it was overthrown by their mismanagement of the war. Valmy, which fell so happily for Brissot and his friends at the moment of their accession to power, was a victory of defence; but for two months afterwards the republican armies advanced across the frontiers carrying "Liberty, Equality, and Fraternity" to Belgians and

Rhine-landers, who did not know what these words meant and soon learnt to associate them with the depredations committed by the armed missionaries of republicanism. In the early days of the Revolution (May 1790), the National Assembly had declared "that the French nation will refuse to undertake any war of conquest, and will never employ its forces against the liberty of any people". But now (November 1792) the Convention published a decree promising brotherly assistance (*fraternité et secours*) to any people wishing to regain its freedom; and a month later another decree regulated "the measures to be taken by French generals in countries occupied by the armies of the republic". The motto was to be "Loot the castle and spare the cottage" (*guerre aux châteaux, paix aux chaumières*). Tithes, taxes, and feudal dues were to be abolished, and all State and public property to be confiscated; whilst "a provisional administration nominated by the people" would confer with French commissioners as to the handing over of the profits to the "Liberators". Thus began the policy of making war pay, which would at the moment make possible the victories of the revolutionary armies, but would contribute largely to their final defeat, when the dislike of French requisitioning, recruiting, and taxation over-balanced the benefits of French "protection" and the fears of French revenge.

Belgium was now in French hands. Valmy (September 20) had been followed by the victory of Jemappes (November 6) and the occupation of Brussels. The decrees of November and December, which followed, not only antagonised the commercial and Catholic Belgians, who saw their banks looted and their church plate melted down, but also alarmed the British Government, which resented nothing so much as the presence of a foreign power on the banks of the Scheldt and the pistol of Antwerp pointed at the heart of London. War with England became at once a probability. Since August 10 there had been no British ambassador in Paris. The September massacre outraged opinion across the Channel. In face of the news from Belgium, Pitt was able to increase the navy and to begin a blockade of the French coast. On the news of the King's execution, which deeply shocked George III, the French ambassador was given his passport. On February 1 the Convention declared war on England, and ten days later Dumouriez invaded Holland.

So long as the war was going well, Robespierre had nothing to say about it; though he still feared defeat, and was alarmed at the counter-revolutionary influence of the *émigrés* and non-juror clergy, and at the growing discontents of the poor. But when public resentment against the occupation of Belgium jeopardised Dumouriez's advance into Holland and forced him to defy the policy of the December decrees, and when on March 18, heavily defeated by the Austrians at Neerwinden, he opened negotiations with the enemy, Robespierre seized the opportunity to discredit the Girondin party and to transfer their power in the Convention to the Jacobins. For the next two months and more hardly a day passed when he did not deliver a harangue in the Assembly or at the Club, driving home every advantage against the "Government." On March 8, when the first certain report came of the dangerous situation in the Netherlands, he even visited one of the most Jacobin *sections* of Paris, and exhorted its members to arm and fly to the help of the army. The meeting ended in such disorder that Brissot accused him of complicity in the abortive rising called "the March days", for the Parisians were already naming their frequent crises after the months when they took place.

Robespierre took this opportunity (March 10) to explain away his indiscretion by a speech which is important for its forecast of Jacobin policy. What was needed, he said, for military victory was centralised control by the Government and discipline on the Home Front. Not merely the personnel but the form of the Government must be changed: let the Assembly delegate its executive powers to a committee of patriots, chosen from its own numbers and representative of all political parties; let them supervise the generals and punish the traitors. Here are the first suggestions of the Committee of Public Safety and the Revolutionary Tribunal. Within a fortnight the Assembly was forced by events to follow Robespierre's lead: for on March 25 it set up a committee of twenty-five deputies of both parties with the title of *commission de salut public* ("The Commission to Save the State"), with power to propose all steps necessary for the defence of the Republic, at home or abroad; it was, in fact, what we should call a Coalition War Cabinet. It was this body which, ten days later (April 6), reduced to ten members, and those all Jacobins, became the famous Committee of Public Safety (*comité de salut public*).

The crisis deepened when Dumouriez, summoned to give up his command, arrested the emissaries of the Convention, handed them over to the Austrians, and tried to march his army on Paris, hoping to dissolve the Assembly and to restore the constitutional monarchy of 1791. But his men refused to follow him, and he galloped off into the enemy's lines. His defection endangered many Girondins; even Robespierre had to explain why he had hitherto trusted the traitor. But his bitterest attacks were reserved for Brissot, whom he now tried to associate with Pitt and the foreign royalist counter-revolutionaries; the easiest and most damaging charge that could be brought against any politician. "Pitt's gold" had for long been a favourite explanation for the royalist intrigues and popular discontents on the home front; and some recent French historians have revived it as a serious cause of the republican reverses—but with singular lack of valid evidence. If the British Government financed a royalist landing in the Vendée, it was an overt act of war; if it maintained an efficient spy service, that was an accepted custom of the diplomatic system; if British bankers speculated in *assignats,* so did Frenchmen. Robespierre's insular mind may have believed that what he said was true; anyhow, it would be effective.

At this critical turn in their fortunes the Girondin party made a fatal move. They indicted Marat on the charge of inciting the people to pillage and murder and of attempting to dissolve the Convention. Robespierre at once insisted that this was an indictment of the whole Jacobin party, of which Marat was in fact an underground and unacknowledged agent. The division on this motion in the Assembly—one of the few in which each deputy proclaimed his vote by name (*appel nominal*)—was quoted afterwards as an easy mode of distinguishing Jacobins from Girondins, and was used with deadly effect in later proscriptions; the trial before a Jacobin court ended in Marat's triumphant acquittal. This was on April 24. A week later (May 1) the Girondins retaliated with an anti-Jacobin demonstration; but the slogan *Vive la loi! A bas la Montagne!* (the Jacobin Left in the Assembly) was easily misrepresented as *Vive le Roi! A bas la République!;* and Robespierre's speech on the 8th eulogised democratic Paris (identified with the Jacobins) at the expense of the supposedly *bourgeois* and Girondin provinces, and proposed a number of measures to arm and organise the People and purge the Government and the country of counter-revolutionaries. The Girondins riposted by setting up a Commission of Twelve to report on the conduct of the Paris Commune; and this body arrested the deputy clerk, Hébert, and other officials of the *municipalité.*

Now was seen the logical result of the events which had brought the National Assembly to Paris. The constitution provided no legal machinery for a Dissolution. A political Opposition which wished to expel the Government and take its place could only appeal to the Sovereign People; in other words, to the armed "active citizens" of the capital. The lesson of July 14 and October 6, 1789, had not been forgotten; neither had the setback of July 17, 1791, nor the triumph of August 10, 1792. It only needed careful and silent preparation amongst the city *sections,* and the force of the National Guard could once more storm the Tuileries—for the Convention had chosen this inauspicious moment (May 10) to move from the crowded *manège* to a spacious hall in the empty palace. During the "March days" an Insurrectional Committee had been formed, on the model of that of August 10. At the beginning of April it took the name of *comité central de salut public,* parodying the parliamentary Committee of Public Safety. Two days after Marat's acquittal, another meeting of sectional delegates at the Mairie (for the Mayor was in the movement) drew up a list of twenty-two Girondin deputies "guilty of the crime of felony against the sovereign people", and demanded their expulsion from the Assembly; but this move was premature. The arrest of officials of the Commune on May 27 gave the insurrectional movement the impulse it needed. Yet another committee, called *comité central révolutionnaire,* was at once forced to plan and carry out the "purging" of the Assembly.

On May 31 Hanriot, the commandant of the National Guard, seized key positions in the city and closed the gates. Prominent Girondins, including Mme Roland, were arrested. A Jacobin majority in the Assembly suppressed the Girondin Commission of Twelve. Next day the Convention was again faced with the demand for the expulsion of the Girondin deputies, and again failed to act. On June 2 they met again, but found the Tuileries surrounded by armed men and gunners, and a vast crowd of citizens, representatives of the Sovereign People. No force was employed or needed: the deputies, like the garrison of the Bastille three years ago, were starved into submission. The Girondin majority could do nothing but accept a Jacobin motion for the suspension and arrest of their leaders.

June 2 was a new kind of revolution—a *coup d'état,* and a bloodless one, almost constitutional. The Jacobin leaders were very proud of it. Paris reckoned that once again the capital had saved the Revolution. Yet it posed more questions than it answered. Was the Convention, when forcibly deprived of so many of its members, any longer National? What kind of constitution would it now provide? Or would the Jacobins, once in power, follow Robespierre's advice, and govern through an executive committee, backed by a summary court? Would the coun-

try as a whole accept the control of a party evidently
Parisian? Had these men the ability and energy, so lacking in their predecessors, to win the war and to suppress
counter-revolution? Would they even be able to control
their allies and masters of the moment—the Paris Commune? These issues had to be faced, and the solution
found for them was the Jacobin regime of 1793–4, commonly but unfairly called the Reign of Terror. But the
victory of June 2 was not yet complete, either at the
centre of government or at the circumference. Five months
intervened before accounts were finally settled with the
Girondin leaders; and Federalism (as the Opposition in
the provinces came to be called) was still not wholly
suppressed when the Jacobins themselves fell a year later.

Paris had for so long been the scene and centre of the
Revolution that the habit had grown up—to which later
historians have been too prone—of ignoring the happenings in the provinces. Yet it had been the peasant revolt
(*jacquerie* and *grande peur*) of 1789 which had inspired
the "abolition of feudalism", the Catholicism of the country-side which had caused the National Assembly to attempt a Church settlement, and the national feeling of
the departments which had given reality to the Fête of
Federation. The townspeople of Varennes had prevented
the King's escape; the *fédérés* of Brest and Marseille had
helped to storm the Tuileries on August 10 and to beat
back the enemy at Valmy on September 20. Some of
these men were as good Jacobins as the Parisians themselves—perhaps better; members of Jacobin clubs in the
commercial cities and ports of the south; subscribers to
Parisian newspapers; members of local Vigilance Committees keeping an eye on aristocrats (*aristos*), non-juror
priests, and other suspects; and of district Directories
trying to administer the confusing decrees about *assignats*
and *émigrés,* food-stuffs and forest-lands that every post
brought from the capital. The danger was that the Paris
deputies, who themselves came from these professional
and *petit bourgeois* classes, might ignore the grievances

of the mass of workers in town and country-side to whom the Revolution had not brought all the blessings they expected of it.

In the big cities of the Medi especially—Lyon, Marseille, Bordeaux—there had been, in kinds and degrees varying with local conditions, "labour troubles", which were aggravated by the outbreak of war, and particularly of war with England, with its coastal blockade and stoppage of imports. In 1789 these places had elected *bourgeois* municipalities in place of the royalist nominees or hereditary officers of the old regime; and these men were of the Girondin type, believers in property, profits, and private enterprise. They hated the "agitators" of the local Jacobin clubs, where emissaries from Paris tried to inflame the workers against their employers, and circulated Robespierre's speeches against the war, or Desmoulins' libellous *Histoire des Brissotins*. When news came of the *coup d'état* of June 2, and some of the escaped Girondin leaders travelled through the provinces preaching vengeance on the Jacobins, Bordeaux, Lyon, Marseille, and Toulon rose in revolt against the government of the Convention, and their leaders talked of a federation of the Midi against Paris and the north not unlike that thought of in 1870 and 1940. The reduction of these places, more by starvation than by military action, and the executions and demolitions with which they were punished, were an unhappy background to the political and constitutional changes which were going on in Paris throughout the summer and autumn of 1793; and the bitterness they engendered goes far to explain the temper of the Jacobin dictatorship.

Robespierre was by nature a peaceful man, a hater of violence and bloodshed; he had declared, after the death of the King, that there should be no more executions. Yet such was his hatred of the men who had led France into war, such his fear of traitors and counter-revolutionaries, and (it may be added) so rapid and apparently painless was death by Dr. Guillotin's new beheading-machine, that he let his conscience be overruled by his reason, and his reason by *raison d'état,* till the Puritan in him became an Inquisitor, and the text of his preaching was "Virtue, without which intimidation [*terreur*] is disastrous, and intimidation, without which virtue has no power".

The "Reign of Terror", then, was a not unnatural outcome of the five months (June–October) during which the Jacobin leaders gradually fastened their hold on a refractory country. Their first step was to win support in the provinces, and to justify their leadership of the Convention by drafting the republican constitution for which France had elected its national deputies. In the eight months since the meeting of the Assembly the Girondins had got no further than the discussion of six out of the 368 articles of Condorcet's too elaborate draft. Within a week of the expulsion of the Girondins (June 9), Hérault de Séchelles produced the "Constitution of 1793", and by the 24th it was passed by the Convention. It was, indeed, as much a Jacobin constitution as Condorcet's would have been a Girondin one; for whilst it promised new "rights" to the people, provided for democratic elections, and encouraged popular revolt against despotism, it also strengthened the executive, and enabled the legislature to deal with urgent matters by decree, without going through the long process of law-making.

The Constitution of 1793 was never enforced: when it had been submitted to a *plébiscite,* and solemnly celebrated in Paris, it was put on the shelf by a decree (October 10) which declared "the provisional government of France revolutionary until the peace". But it remained on the statute-book, with all the gaps and faults due to its hasty composition, as a Jacobin ideal; and the demand for its introduction played a part in most of the later attacks upon the regime of the Terror.

The twenty-nine Girondins expelled from the Convention on June 2 were placed under nominal arrest; but twenty of them escaped into the provinces. These men found it easy to exploit the economic and religious discontents of the Midi and the Vendée, till sixty departments of the south and west were in revolt against Paris and twenty-one departments of the centre and north-west. It was a civil war; but one in which the capital had a military advantage, and the Government could win popular support by higher salaries for officials and easier sales of national land. When on July 13, Charlotte Corday, a Caen girl who had been worked upon by Girondin propaganda, came to Paris and murdered Marat, the Jacobins seized the opportunity to outlaw the Girondin leaders who were now at large, and to bring to trial those who were still in their hands. After a trial which lasted six days, and in which Girondism was identified with every failure or heresy of the Revolution, nineteen Girondins, including Brissot, Gensonné, and Vergniaud, went to the scaffold (October 31). The rest were hunted down in the provinces, and, if caught, executed without trial; or they died by their own hands—Pétion on the Spanish frontier, Roland by the roadside near Rouen, when he heard of his wife's execution. Of sixty-three leaders of the party of "Liberals and idealists", only twenty-five survived the Revolution.

The Girondins rose and fell for much the same reasons as the philosophical Radicals of the 1830s: excess of theory, deficiency of practice; reliance upon persuasion and reason, distrust of compulsion and control; with a liking for men of property and intelligence, and too little understanding of the man in the street. Every revolution is the poorer if it repudiates (as it so often does) its men of culture and enlightenment. But the Girondins had shown no generosity to their opponents, and they died with bitterness in their hearts. They had failed to govern the country, and France does not easily forgive failure.

Chapter 6

The Jacobin Regime

LOUIS XVI WAS DEAD and France had no king. Its ruler was the Sovereign People. But it could not escape from a pattern of government which had been traditional for a thousand years. Both National Assemblies—the Constituent, which made the Constitution of 1791, and the Legislative, which destroyed it—had carried on the government of the country through ministers appointed by the crown and a Civil Service (as we should call it) centralised in the capital. True, there had gone with this an extremely decentralised local administration, in place of the old *intendants*. But this experiment had failed; and the frequency with which deputies or "national agents" were sent into the provinces to explain the views of the Government, or to purge the local authorities of unworthy members, showed how Paris clung to the monarchical tradition. Both these Assemblies had, in their distrust of the King's ministers and in their desire to rule, elected standing committees to supervise and if necessary overrule the policy of the ministries; foreign policy, in particular, had depended more upon Mirabeau than Montmorin in 1790, and more upon Brissot than Delessart in 1791. It was not likely that the Convention would break with this tradition; it, too, set up no less than twenty-one such committees, with an average of twenty-four members, concerning themselves with every department of government.

But things were very different from what they had been in the previous Assemblies. On May 10, 1793, only three weeks before the expulsion of the Girondin deputies, the Assembly had moved from the riding-school (*manège*) to the old theatre (*salle des machines*) of the Tuileries— a much roomier and more dignified debating-place. But, whether designedly or not, the deputies no longer sat on two sides of a narrow chamber, like our House of Commons, but in a semi-circle of seats all facing towards the rostrum. The President became a schoolmaster and every speaker a lecturer. There was no longer a Right and a Left; members could no more "cross the floor of the House". Though the upper block of seats at one end of the semi-circle, occupied by the Paris deputies, might be nicknamed the Mountain (*la Montagne*), and the undistinguished majority of the centre might still be called the Marsh (*marais*), the old easy antagonism was destroyed; and a democratic parliament was half-way to becoming, what it is in totalitarian countries, a mere audience, all facing the same way. Nor was this change superficial. It signified an innovation: a new experiment, which was at the same time a renovation, a return to old ways in parliamentary government. In the crisis of the spring of 1793—the King's execution, the outbreak of war with England, Dumouriez's defeat and desertion—a new kind of committee had been appointed, called at first *comité de défense générale,* then *comité de salut public,* with power to take any steps necessary for the safety of the country. With the death of the King, the continuance of the crisis into the summer, and the deadly struggle between two political factions, it was likely that the successful party would try to perpetuate a committee with such wide executive powers, and would use it to overrule the Assembly and to govern the country. That was what happened.

The Committee of Public Safety of April 6, 1793, originally consisted of nine Jacobins, of whom two, Barère and Lindet, became permanent members. At the end of May it was increased temporarily to fourteen members; but again reduced to nine on July 10, when Danton was excluded. Robespierre was not added till July 27. Four additional members, including Carnot, brought the total up to twelve by September 6; and these were re-elected monthly until the fall of the Jacobin government ten months later. For the Committee was nominally representative of the Convention, and could at any time be dismissed by it; and if it ruled by fear, it also ruled by

success. It was a Cabinet, but a Cabinet without a Premier. During working hours, which were from 8 a.m. to
10 p.m. every day of the week, its members shared out
the ministerial departments; they met in the evening to
report, discuss, and sign documents. The Committee kept
no minutes, and the only record of its work consists of
copies of its resolutions and decrees; from the comparison
of the handwriting and signatures of these documents,
some rather precarious evidence can be drawn as to the
responsibilities of its various members.

Lazare Carnot was a soldier with a professional train-
ing in military schools which were so good that British
officers went to France to learn their business: a patriot,
who cared about nothing but winning the war, and would
stand up to Bonaparte if he thought he knew a better
way of doing so. For assistant in managing the armies
he had Prieur, deputy for the Côte d'Or, author of a book
on military science and inventor of the decimal system.
With them was associated Robert Lindet, a quartermaster-
general of genius, with a roving commission over the
whole field of supply. Naval affairs were under Saint-
André, an ex-Protestant preacher and captain in the
merchant navy. Billaud-Varenne, an actor, and Collot
d'Herbois, a dramatist, had both deserted the stage for
politics, risen to Presidency of the Convention, and been
elected on to the Committee to silence their opposition
to its policy; they represented the popular party of violence. A second Prieur, deputy for la Marne, was a tried
republican and administrator, generally absent from Paris
on missions on behalf of the Committee. This was often
so with two other members who were close friends of
Robespierre: Couthon and Saint-Just. Couthon was almost the same age, a lawyer too, a fanatic, and a cripple,
whose wheeled-chair may still be seen in a Paris museum.
Saint-Just, the youngest member of the Committee (he
was only twenty-six in 1793), had been rescued from idle
and even criminal ways by his enthusiasm for Robespierre,
and was now his most devoted follower, prepared to face
any sacrifice for "the cause". There remains Barère, whose

constant presence and readiness to undertake any business from diplomacy to the Fine Arts made him indispensable; but a trimmer and a time-server. To these ten must be added the name of Hérault de Séchelles, the author of the Constitution of 1793; but he remained only nine months on the Committee, fell under suspicion of treachery, and was executed along with the Dantonists on April 5, 1794.

What did Robespierre, the twelfth member, think of his associates? There was not much in them that appealed to him, unless it were Carnot's patriotism, Couthon's stoicism, and the fanatical youthfulness of Saint-Just. The business of war he disliked; the business of intimidation he preferred to conduct in his own way. He was invited to come on the Committee because no one had so much experience of the Revolution, or so much influence at the Jacobin Club, or carried so much weight as an orator. His opposition would have been fatal; his presence provided a planner, a parliamentarian, and a popular hero. His colleagues did not all like his plans, especially the stress he laid on virtue and religion; some of them were conscious of his inquisitorial eye upon them; most of them thought his pose as a prophet and martyr of republicanism insufferable, and resented his superior airs and intolerances. Theirs was an uncomfortable association, held together less by sympathy than by the necessity for hard work in a common task. They were like a group of shipwrecked mariners or arctic explorers, whose forced intimacy begets unexpected irritations, but with the added friction of long hours, no holidays, and the noise and stress of city life.

Robespierre left no memoirs, and his infrequent letters are seldom self-revealing; but there was found amongst his papers after his death a small notebook (carnet) containing rough memoranda on matters to be brought up at the Committee (or perhaps the Convention or the Club) during the last three months of 1793. They deal with so many subjects that it would be tempting to think of Robespierre as a kind of Prime Minister, were there any direct evidence that anyone held such a position.

Rather they suggest that he was a "Minister without portfolio", who was tied to no departmental desk and might interest himself in all the work of the Committee. The knowledge he thus acquired was naturally used in the speeches he made in the Convention introducing Government business, or at the Club commending the policy of the Committee to the Paris electors and the world at large. He thus held the stage as the spokesman and figurehead of the Jacobin government; and though he had no ambition or fitness for personal dictatorship, he came to be regarded in France, and in foreign countries too, as the real head of a dictatorial committee.

The original reference of the Committee had been "to supervise and speed up the administration in charge of the Provisional Executive Council," i.e. the Ministers provisionally appointed by the Assembly on August 10, 1792. It was authorised "in urgent circumstances, to take measures of general defence, both internal and external". It could draw on the Treasury for secret expenses. It soon had power to arrest "all persons suspected or warned". Before the end of the year it controlled not only the ministers but also the generals and administrative authorities, and received constant reports from councils, courts, and military headquarters all over the country—reports which, if they had been duly rendered and carefully read, might have made the Committee as omniscient as it was omnicompetent. The only limitations to its power were the monthly re-election of its members by the Convention, its financial dependence on the Treasury, and the privilege by which deputies could not be arrested without consent of the Assembly.

It was assisted but also hampered in its disciplining of officials and searching out of suspects by a rival body called the Committee of General Security, a Standing Committee with police functions, set up six months before it (October 17, 1792), and more than once reconstituted, but now consisting of fourteen members, who also were re-elected monthly until the fall of the Jacobins in July 1794. The fourteen members of the Police Committee were older men than the twelve of the Political Committee, as the other, from contrast of its functions, might well be called. Only four of them were Parisians. They had a big staff, dealing with the suspects of eighty-four departments. Their origin and interests made them more conservative and provincial than their brother Jacobins of the younger committee, and they were not unnaturally jealous of its constantly growing authority. This feeling came to a head when the Political Committee entrusted its own powers of arrest, especially over errant officials of the Government, to a sub-committee called *Bureau de police générale* (March 17, 1794); it might happen that one committee released persons the other had arrested, and vice versa. This was a serious flaw in the flywheel of the Government machine.

The committee pattern of organisation, so congenial to a popular movement, was not confined to the Government or the capital. Even before the Revolution there had been exceptions to the rule that the French provinces had no life of their own, and took their political opinions, as they nowadays take their fashions of dress, from Paris. Not a few departmental capitals had their university and their academy; in most of the larger towns there were groups of citizens who subscribed to a Paris paper, or met in a reading-room (*salon de lecture*) to discuss the news of the day. When the Revolution broke out, it was noticed that such discussions became more and more political, and that the leaders of local Jacobinism were largely the same men as had attended the reading-room or belonged to the Masonic Lodge. Electors in 1789, members of the popularly appointed municipalities in 1790 or 1791, they supplied the nucleus of the local Jacobin clubs, of which there were some 200 at the end of 1790 and at least 3,000 by 1793–4. The word "club" had been borrowed from England early in the eighteenth century, and used of any association of like-minded people for literary or cultural purposes; but the Revolution gave it a political turn—a Jacobin club was as unlike Boodle's or Brookes's as anything could well be; it existed solely for debating purposes. But it was founded by "Patriots", and as revolutionary opinion moved towards the Left, it turned out its Girondin members, became a Jacobin preserve, and translated its principles into practice: it circulated copies of Robespierre's speeches, and sent up to the parent society in Paris, at critical moments, addresses of congratulation and loyalty. It was often closely associated, if not identified, with a Popular Society (*société populaire*) or Vigilance Committee (*comité de surveillance*), whose members made it more particularly their business to purge the local authorities of reactionary elements, or to track down and imprison refractory clergy, friends of *émigrés*, or other suspected persons.

These local cells of Jacobinism played an important part in the rout of the Girondins and "Federalists", who had no urge or flair for such propaganda; but their vagaries and extravagances often embarrassed the Government. The remedy it employed was an extension of a practice already employed by the Constituent and Legislative Assemblies—that of sending deputies round the country, particularly to their own part of the world, as *représentants en mission,* to explain the views of the Government and to standardise local administration. In the spring of 1793 the Convention had despatched deputies to every department to raise recruits, and had attached three with wide powers to every army at the front. Before long, national agents (*agents nationaux*)—no longer independent deputies, but officials employed by the Government—travelled on roving commissions through the provinces, whilst military commissioners (*commissaires aux armées*) went to the front with the generals, reported on their doings to the Government, and even led their troops in the field. In this way a hand-to-mouth centralisation was imposed on the decentralised pattern of the Revolution. Under the stress of war and economic conditions the New Order was slipping back into the Old, and the Committee of Public Safety found itself forced to revive the methods of the Bourbon monarchy, which had been so recently anathematised and overthrown.

With this machinery under its hand, the Committee of Public Safety proceeded to put into force its policy for the Home Front. This had been outlined by Robespierre in a series of notes which were apparently written when he came on to the Committee in July 1793, and which were published after his death by Courtois, the hostile editor of his papers: he called them, not unfairly, a Catechism.

What is our aim?
It is the use of the Constitution for the benefit of the people.
Who are likely to oppose us?
The rich and the corrupt.
What methods will they employ?
Slander and hypocrisy.
What factors will encourage the use of such means?
The ignorance of the *sansculottes* (i.e. the workers).
The people must therefore be instructed.
What obstacles are there to its enlightenment?
The paid journalists, who mislead it every day by shameless impostures.
What conclusion follows?
That we ought to proscribe these writers as the most dangerous enemies of the country, and to circulate an abundance of good literature.
What other obstacle is there to the instruction of the people?
Its poverty.
When, then, will the people be educated?
When it has enough bread to eat, and when the rich and the Government cease bribing treacherous pens and tongues to deceive it; when their interests are identified with those of the people.
When will this be?
Never.
What other obstacles are there [*he goes on, after this lapse into pessimism*] to the achievement of freedom?
The war at home and abroad.

By what means can the foreign war be ended?
By placing republican generals at the head of our armies, and by punishing those who have betrayed us.
How can we end the civil war?
By punishing traitors and conspirators, especially those deputies and administrators who are to blame; by sending patriot troops under patriot leaders to reduce the aristocrats of Lyon, Marseille, Toulon, the Vendée, the Jura, and all other districts where the banner of royalism and rebellion has been raised; and by making a terrible example of all the criminals who have outraged liberty, and spilt the blood of patriots.

A Catechism, certainly, in its form; in its matter a programme; and in Robespierre's own mind a self-examination paper by which he tested, from time to time, the progress of the Jacobin government towards his ideal republic of liberty and virtue. Each had three headings: the Constitution; the Press; Poverty.

First, the use of the Constitution for the benefit of the people. At the moment (July 1793), Hérault's *Constitution of 1793* had just been accepted by the Convention, and a few days later its enactment was celebrated by a public fête: but Robespierre had never been wholly satisfied with it, and soon persuaded himself that the dangerous state of affairs at home and abroad—the victory of Wattignies came only on October 16, the execution of the Girondins on October 31, and the fall of Toulon not till the end of the year—made it impossible to hold general elections, to inaugurate a new Assembly, and to risk a change of government. He and his colleagues were convinced (as so many provisional governments have been) that it was a "transitional period" during which their continuance in office was necessary for the sake of the country, and that when peace was restored at home and abroad their constitutional promises could be carried out, and they would thankfully hand over their heavy responsibilities to worthier successors. Meanwhile they would suffer no opposition, and would repress any movement for a premature return to democratic institutions. How far their trusteeship of national rights fell short of plain dictatorship most of them were too busy to inquire, though there are indications that Robespierre himself became increasingly troubled by such doubts.

It was the Revolution itself that had created the problem of the press. Before 1789 hardly half a dozen papers were in circulation in Paris or the provinces, and their subscribers were an educated élite. Mirabeau's *Etats-généraux,* the first attempt to print accounts of the debates at Versailles, was at once prohibited; but the ban could not be enforced; within a fortnight fresh papers were licensed, and soon there were so many in the cafés and on the streets that almost every prominent politician seemed to have his own journal—two to four pages only, for the most part, appearing once or twice a week, with a few items of foreign news, garbled versions of parliamentary proceedings, and leading articles (there were the essential feature) giving the political views of the editor. Nowadays it costs millions to start and carry on a daily paper. Then it could be done by any deputy—Robespierre was one—out of the savings of his parliamentary salary of £5 a week. And since there was no censorship, no law of libel, and no longer any fear of summary imprisonment under a *lettre de cachet,* there was no limit to the misrepresentations and personal scurrility of some of these papers. The best of them, indeed, made some attempt to report the speeches in the Assembly, giving most space to the politicians of their own party. Seats were reserved for reporters; but shorthand had not been invented, and it was not easy, with the best will in the world, to give an accurate account of the debates: for an important speech it was not unusual to borrow the orator's manuscript afterwards. For France, nowadays generally regarded as a home of ready orators contrasted with tongue-tied Britons, could then hardly produce an extempore speaker, and the debates in the National Assembly were not to be compared, for eloquence and argument, with those in the House of Commons. Only when the written essays had been read, and formal debate gave way to interludes of personal altercation, did the proceedings excite the paid *claqueurs* in the public galleries.

The circulation of these papers was not often more than 2,000–5,000 copies; but it was worth while for the victors of August 10 to raid the royalist presses, and confiscate their type; and the same thing happened to the Girondin papers in June 1793. It became a favourite method of Jacobin propaganda to subsidise Hébert's popular *Père Duchesne,* and to distribute it amongst the troops at the front; it is said to have reached a circulation of a million. The press played its part again in the break-up of the Jacobin government: Desmoulins' *Vieux Cordelier* cost him his life. Robespierre, then, was not wrong in insisting upon the power of the press, even in a country which was some 80 per cent. illiterate, as a main political factor.

Robespierre was equally convinced as to the political power of the stage. In the franchise debates of October 1789 he had championed the rights of actors against the old Catholic prejudice which regarded them as "untouchables": "their virtues [he maintained] would reform the stage, and the theatres would become schools of high principles, good behaviour, and patriotism". Soon actors were given citizens' rights, the censorship of the stage was lifted, and the theatres seized the opportunity to put on a series of plays on historical or political subjects, in which every topical allusion was cheered or hissed by partisans in the pit. When the Jacobins came into power they found it advisable to re-establish a censorship of the stage; some plays were banned as "tending to deprave public opinion, or to revive the shameful superstition of royalism"; others of an edifying character were staged by Government order as a counter-blast.

These were simple problems, perhaps, compared to the third remedy on Robespierre's list—the alleviation of poverty. His thought on this subject was more prophetic than is generally allowed. As against the *bourgeois* deputy who thought only of "workmen" and "wages", or the

Catholic priest who found the poor and outcast easier to
save than the respectable, he believed, like any modern
Fabian, that "poverty is a crime"; and he would have
welcomed the hard conclusion of *Major Barbara* that it
is only when the people as a whole is free from economic
depression and social subordination that it will be fit for
salvation—and then a new religion will be needed to save
it. In more than one speech delivered when the Constitution of 1793 was in the making he had laid undue stress,
perhaps, upon the Rights of Man; this was natural enough,
since they had been so newly recognised. But he had
always thought more of their moral than of their legal
implications. "Man is born for happiness and freedom,"
he had declared on May 10, 1793. "The object of society
is the preservation of his rights, *and the perfecting of his
nature.*" If he constantly insists upon the need of safe-
guards against misgovernment, it is because the governors
are not yet identified with the governed. If he nevertheless
accepts a regime of centralised control and force, it is in
the hope that it is transitional to a state in which France
will be one people, one faith, and one will, embodied in
a peaceful and law-abiding society, in a government that
realises the rights of man, and in a Church that worships
the God of Nature.

But how, *how* was this to be brought about? Robespierre found himself involved, as any idealist might, in
a hundred difficult problems of property and profits, rent
and wages, housing and unemployment—every townsman
knew something about these; and in the older and ob-
scurer rights and wrongs of the country-side—those questions of different kinds of tenure, of common lands and
enclosure, of rotation of crops and fallow, of grazing
rights and the reclamation of marsh-lands, of which most
of the deputies knew little, and which still puzzle historians. Moreover, the two classes of problem were con-
nected and complicated by the long-standing feud between
the village producer and the town consumer, fought out
in every market-place of the country, each of which might

have its own prices, as it had its own weights and measures.

Although under the old regime the common people of Paris were reputed to be peaceful and amenable to order (an order enforced by occasional public executions in the Place de Grève), yet signs had not been wanting during the early months of the Revolution—the Réveillon riot (April 1789), the murder of Foullon and Berthier (July 1789), or of the baker François (October 1789)—that their temper was changing. But it was enough, for the first three years of the new regime, to keep the policing of the capital in middle-class hands (only "active" citizens were admitted to the National Guard), and to use the *Loi le Chapelier* to repress any attempts by the workers to agitate for better conditions of labour. There was as yet little evidence that the teeming slums of the *faubourg Saint-Antoine* were a political danger. The fall of the Bastille, the march to Versailles, the attack on the Tuileries, the expulsion of the Girondin deputies, had been the work of the small tradesmen and artisans, the *sansculottes* (as all citizens who wore democratic trousers instead of aristocratic breeches might be called), but not of the "rabble" (*la canaille*); though a few of these, bribed by money or drink, might bring up the rear. But one of the decrees passed by the Insurrectional Commune of August 10, 1792, abolished "passive" citizenship, and from about this time some *sections* of the city admitted hitherto disfranchised citizens to their meetings and to their battalions of the National Guard. This innovation increased the tension between the Convention, which was still *bourgeois* (it only included two genuine working men), and the Commune and sectional committees, on which the "workers" (the *bras nus,* as a recent writer has called them) were increasingly represented.

This development certainly put an unexpected strain on Robespierre's belief in the Divine Right of the common people. What was to be done, in face of the growing power of the disfranchised, the dispossessed? Relief works for the unemployed (*ateliers de charité*) had been tried, and condemned; for they only attracted wastrels from the country-side. The munitions factories set up during the war provided employment for many thrown out of the old luxury trades. Better housing for the poor was not thought of, if, indeed, it was ever demanded; nor control of rents. The feeding of Paris, on the other hand, was, as it had always been, a constant anxiety to the Government. Grain and vegetables were drawn from all the country round; meat from farther afield; and both had to be supplemented by foreign imports. Any local failure of crops, any outbreak of civil disorder in the provinces, any hostile blockading of the seaports, even a lowering of the level of the Seine that put the water-mills out of order, might mean bread-queues and food-riots. At Christmas, 1793, the *administration des subsistances* introduced bread rationing by means of food coupons, and a few months later meat rationing too. Good meals could still be procured at the restaurants, but only at a price beyond most patriotic purses. It was the common belief—in an age that knew little of economics—that the food shortages were due to hoarders (*accapareurs*) and speculators (*agioteurs*), encouraged by English bribery ("Pitt's gold") to ruin the republic; and in the autumn of 1793 an *armée révolutionnaire* recruited in the capital (Robespierre was one of its sponsors) set out to coerce farmers and shop-keepers to produce the needed supplies.

But this was only a temporary concession to the Commune. The serious and long-term attempt of the Jacobins to deal with the food problem was the so-called *maximum,* or system of price-control. The first experiment in this direction was the decree of May 4, 1793, forced upon the Girondin government just before its fall. It fixed a maximum price for grain in each department, and obliged farmers to make a return of their stocks and to sell them in the open market. Soon the plan was extended. A decree of September 29, under the Jacobin government, fixed maximum prices (varying from market to market) for nearly fifty commodities, including clothes and tobacco. But the attempt to enforce the law was defeated by the depreciation of the currency, by wartime requisitioning of supplies for the armies, and by hoarding, black-marketing, and other such practices, which no system of control was ever strong enough to suppress. The radical vice of these measures was, of course, the failure to fix the same prices for the whole country; this could not be done. Even the revised and final scheme of March 1794 did no more than fix local prices at the level of 1790, plus five per cent. for the producer, ten per cent. for the retailer, and the cost of transport to the capital of the district— an arrangement too evidently designed in the interest of the manufacturer and middleman. Nor was the poor consumer consoled when he learnt that the corollary of price-control was to be wages-control; the *maximum des salaires* had no little to do with the downfall of the Jacobin government.

All these devices left the basic problem of poverty almost untouched. Under the old regime the poor man was at least a proper subject for feudal protection and the charity of the Church. But this privilege of pauperism had disappeared with its patrons; and if poverty was now a crime, the State must find some means to deal with it. The Constitution of 1793 had grandly announced (Article 21) that the relief of the poor was the first duty of the State (*Les secours publics sont une dette sacrée*), and that society must provide a living for persons in distress, either by finding them work, or by supporting them if they are unemployable; and there was a serious attempt to carry out this promise. An annual grant was made to the departmental authorities, to be used in providing genuine paupers with paid employment, outdoor relief, or a place in an institution; meanwhile, mere mendicants were either to be imprisoned or transported. Assistance was given to mothers in childbirth, boys were apprenticed, old people pensioned, and family allowances given for more than two children. Barère's *livre de bienfaisance nationale* (a kind of Beveridge Plan, co-ordinating previous experiments) allowed each department to draw up a list of persons qualified to receive pensions or sickness benefits; with an additional list of mothers and widows entitled to special relief. But as these were waiting lists, with only 600 names at a time for each department, the annual *Fête de malheur* at which the beneficiaries were expected to celebrate the generosity of the State was not likely to be overcrowded. Robespierre's young disciple Saint-Just had another scheme which appeared on the statute-book as the *Laws of Ventôse;* but it was no more effective than Barère's. He proposed that the property of all political prisoners should be confiscated and distributed among the poor. But how far would the assets of 80,000 prisoners go (if there were so many) towards satisfying the needs of the poor of 40,000 communes? The plan proved unworkable and died with its author, who had perhaps thought of it as a first step towards a systematic transference of wealth from the rich to the poor.

The interest of these experiments lies in their antici-pation of later measures. They failed because France was not an economic whole; because the politicians had no social statistics to draw upon; and because the country was at war, its ports and frontiers blockaded, its currency of no purchasing value. Could the failure be redeemed in other ways? By creating a state of "full employment" in the armies, the munitions factories, and the fields? By holding to ransom, not merely the *émigrés,* aristocrats, and other counter-revolutionary classes in the country, but also the "re-united" and "liberated" peoples outside it, on the pattern of Belgium, Luxemburg, or Savoy? By carrying the war overland and overseas, founding tribu-tary republics in Italy and a colonial Empire in Egypt? Would the politicians, after all, be saved by the army and navy? In these, as in many other respects, Napoleon in-herited the goodwill of the Revolution.

Robespierre took little interest in the republican navy, beyond helping to abolish the brutal punishments which had been common under the old regime, and hoping for the removal of royalist officers. This was more difficult than in the army, where only gunnery and engineering required such specialised knowledge as was needed by every naval officer. For two years after 1789 aristocrat officers commanded French ships with royalist names, and flew the Bourbon white flag with a small tricolor in the corner. It was only by degrees that commissions were given to men from the lower deck or from the merchant navy. With Jeanbon Saint-André, himself a sea captain, at the Admiralty, this process went on; but though Villaret-Joyeuse won credit at the battle of the First of June 1794, the amateurishness and indiscipline of an extemporised navy could never recover the supremacy won by the expert admirals and shipbuilders of the pre-revolutionary period. If young Bonaparte had chosen the navy instead of the army for his profession, as he nearly did, things might have been different.

Two heads of Robespierre's "Catechism" remain. He believed that the foreign war could be ended by the appointment of "patriot" generals, and the civil war by the punishment of traitors. *Sancta simplicitas!* It was the programme of a provincial lawyer whose family had no military traditions, and of a fanatical revolutionary whose world was bisected into patriots and traitors.

In the Constituent Assembly Robespierre had more than once shown that he did not believe in military discipline, and resented the harsh punishments of the old army. In the debate about the formation of the National Guard he wanted this "new army" to be as little as possible like the old: not a professional force, with an *élite* of officers, always in uniform, a class apart, but a volunteer army, the nation in arms. He feared "royalist" officers, and would have dismissed them all; but he feared militarism more, under whatever leaders: "there must be no attempt to turn our men into machines". His opposition to Brissot's war policy in the Legislative Assembly of 1791 was based on his fear of a military dictatorship— a fear partly justified by the history of Dumouriez and Lafayette, and wholly by that of Bonaparte.

When war broke out he defined more clearly in the *Défenseur* his ideas about military discipline. An army, he admitted, could not exist without it; but one is first a man, secondly a citizen, and thirdly a soldier; military discipline need not be enforced outside the barracks, or off the field of battle. Such theories were soon disproved by experience. The victory of Valmy was made possible by the unexpected steadiness of the volunteer troops under fire; but it was won by the artillery of the old royalist army. In the successful campaign that followed, the professionalism of the old army was happily partnered by the amateurism of the new; it was not till Dumouriez's retreat from Holland brought out the quarrels between the soldiers and the politicians that the question of army reorganisation was seriously faced. Already, in January 1793, Dubois-Crancé, a regular officer who had served in the republican forces, had brought forward a scheme for recruiting 300,000 volunteers, and creating eight armies, to serve on the various fronts; he afterwards added a plan called the *amalgame*, by which veterans were to be mixed with recruits in the proportion of one to three, and the men were to choose their own officers. Soon commissioned "rankers" and regular officers—such as Bonaparte himself—were serving side by side, and a marshal's baton might be found either in a patriot's knapsack or in a desk at the *école militaire*. This pattern of military service was carried on under the "mass levies" of 1793 and 1794, and the modified conscription of the *loi Jourdan* (1797). Thus was created the Grand Army of Napoleon.

But it was a long time before the suspicion of "royalist" officers died down. Robespierre's demand for "patriot" generals, strengthened by the defection of Lafayette in 1792 and Dumouriez in 1793, soon became a demand for "Jacobin" generals. During that summer, with the Robespierrist Bouchotte at the War Office, a clean sweep was made of aristocrat officers. It was not easy to replace them; the drunken Rossignol was no credit to his patrons; Carteaux (an ex-artist) and Doppet (an ex-journalist) had to be replaced by the veteran Dugommier before Bonaparte's guns could force the British to retreat from Toulon. Bonaparte himself was nearly executed as a

Robespierrist (and therefore at the moment not a "patriot") in the Thermidorian reaction of 1794.

Yet, setting absurdities aside, the republican armies of 1793–4 were an astonishing fact. Carnot's decree of August 1793 declared that "the republic is a great city in a state of siege: France must become one vast camp, and Paris its arsenal. . . . Every Frenchman is commandeered for the needs of the armies. Young men will go to the front: married men will forge arms and carry food: women will make tents and clothing, and work in hospitals: children will turn old linen into bandages: old men will be carried into the squares to rouse the courage of the combatants, and to teach hatred of kings, and republican unity". The republican armies, the outcome of this national effort, made little pretence to the fine appearance and disciplined movements of the regiments which had last fought (and been defeated) in the Seven Years War. Their commanders, if they had not read their Guibert, had at least learnt how to make the best use of numbers and of French *élan*. The general rules laid down in Carnot's army order of February 1794 were "always to manœuvre *en masse* and on the offensive; to maintain strict but not too detailed discipline; to keep the troops in constant readiness, without over-working them; to employ the utmost watchfulness on sentry-go; to use the bayonet on every possible occasion; and to follow up the enemy without pause until he is completely destroyed". It only needed a leader of genius to carry such armies across Europe. These men were more sensibly dressed than their British opponents; marched faster, and knew better how to live on the land; their infantry did not shoot so straight, and were overborne by bigger and stronger men in the hand-to-hand *mêlée* in which most battles ended; their cavalry were worse mounted, but did not behave as though they were following hounds.

It was part of Robespierre's creed, and the conviction of his colleagues on the Committee of Public Safety, that the two wars—foreign and civil—were in reality one, and that the corollary of the appointment of "patriot" generals was the punishment of domestic traitors. If a national war diverts public attention from misgovernment and weakens the power of political minorities, it also increases the risk from such leaders of discontent as remain at large. There was nothing fanciful in this fear during the summer of 1793, when Lyon, Marseille, Toulon, Bordeaux, and the Vendée were in armed revolt against the Jacobin government of Paris, the ruling party in their own National Convention. A civil war is generally more merciless than any other, and the military executions of the west, the mass-shooting of rebels at Lyon or Toulon, and the savage decrees which struck the names of Lyon and Marseille off the map of France, are at least understandable in the emergency of the moment. Yet these things were by no means the whole Reign of Terror—indeed, they are wrongly included in it. Robespierre himself protested against the terrorist crimes of Carrier at Nantes and Fouché at Lyon; but he had no qualms about the proceedings of the Revolutionary Tribunal, which, according to its own official returns, between January 1793 and June 1795 sent 2,795 persons to the guillotine. These were for the most part ordinary citizens convicted, after formal trial, of offences against the State and the laws of the republic.

Side by side with the regular system of courts trying civil and criminal cases, there had existed, ever since August 10, 1792, a *tribunal extraordinaire,* afterwards called *révolutionnaire,* with special jurisdiction over *political* crimes; what might nowadays be called a People's Court. This Revolutionary Tribunal sat only in Paris, though its victims included, besides persons under arrest in the prisons of the capital, others sent up from time to time from the provinces; and ultimately it was given jurisdiction over all political cases. Its judges were appointed by the State; its public prosecutor put the case for the Government; its jurymen were permanent officials; prisoners were allowed to speak in their own defence, but generally could not find counsel to act for them; witnesses were heard but seldom cross-examined; the verdict went by a majority in the jury; the sentence—acquittal, imprisonment, deportation, or death—was at the discretion of the presiding judge. The court held its trials in public; but the common assumption was that anyone the Government put on trial was guilty, and it was only upon rare occasions that the eloquence or attractive looks of a defendant won the favour of the audience and the votes of the jury.

Yet it is a mistake to suppose that few of the prisoners were acquitted. During the five winter months of 1793–4 some 750 were condemned and 500 acquitted. It is also wrong to think that the victims were all "priests or aristocrats". Such, perhaps, were most of the original inmates of the Paris prisons and the earliest to be brought to trial; but during the three months of the Tribunal's busiest activity (April to June 1794), the number of clergy and nobles executed was 225, of officers and officials 262, and of civilian members of the middle and lower classes— clerks, shop-keepers, inn-keepers, labourers, and so forth —617. The meaning of these figures is that a court originally set up to deal with an emergency, and to liquidate political traitors, came to be used as a convenient method by which the Government could enforce its will on the country without going through the ordinary forms of justice.

Robespierre was a member of this Government and accepted its methods. As lately as January 1793 he had expressed his dislike of capital punishment, and had said he hoped the execution of the King would be the last use of it. But two months later, during the Dumouriez crisis, he declared that it should be the penalty for "every attempt made against the security of the State, or the liberty, equality, unity, and indivisibility of the republic". A few months later again he was for bringing before the Tribunal the "aristocrat" Custine and other unsuccessful generals. His *carnet* shows that at the end of this year he was concerned about the working of the Tribunal, and in favour of concentrating all political trials in Paris. He would remain dissatisfied with it until the drastic laws of April and June 1794 swept away the last obstacles to its "purge of traitors". Are we to attribute this change of view to a moral deterioration in Robespierre's character? Or to the silencing of private conscience in a man unaccustomed to public responsibilities? Or to the fanatical passion of an Inquisitor who thinks that by sacrificing the body he can save the soul of the State? Many answers were given by Robespierre's contemporaries: some thought him a hypocrite, some a patriot, some a fiend. It is likely enough that he could not have found a clear answer himself in that twisted, tortured, yet complacent mind of his. The historian can only say that the balance of evidence drawn from his letters and speeches favours the view that he was a moral fanatic, who deliberately used means he would ordinarily have disliked to attain ends that he always valued above any immediate popularity or power: a Cromwell, but without his soldierly directness; a Calvin, but without his cramping theology.

The regime called the Reign of Terror—a bureaucratic dictatorship of control and intimidation—was the work of the whole Committee of Public Safety, backed by the votes of the Convention, and accepted by the mass of public opinion; witness the monthly re-election of the Committee, the congratulatory addresses from the provinces, the absence of any demonstrations in favour of the victims of the guillotine. It was not till the deputies themselves were threatened, till the "purge" spread to local Jacobin clubs, and till the man in the street found his petty hoarding and profiteering treated as political crimes, that public opinion could be moved to make an end of the Tribunal, and of the men who had used it to keep themselves in power.

Chapter 7

The Reign of Terror

As 1793 MOVED INTO 1794 it soon became evident—and not least to Robespierre, the acutest of the Jacobin leaders—that the second year of the republic (*An*. II had begun on September 22, 1793) would have troubles of its own not less serious than those of the previous twelve months. It might have been thought that with the execution of the King (January 21), the Queen (October 16), and Princess Elisabeth (May 10), and the close imprisonment of the Dauphin and his sister in the Temple, all danger of a royalist reaction was over; that Girondism had finally perished with its leaders and amidst the ruins of "federal" Lyon and Marseille; and that the victory of Wattignies (October 16) had ended the "war against Kings." Why should not France now relax and enjoy the blessings of peace under the democratic republic provided for in the Constitution of 1783? Robespierre and his colleagues on the Committee did not think this could be done; and the Jacobin regime went on towards the downfall that every incident of the next six months made more inevitable. It would be easy to say that the Jacobins were in love with power, or that Robespierre established a personal dictatorship: the first statement would be partly true, the second mostly false; neither would really explain what happened.

Royalism was not dead, so long as the young Dauphin ("Louis XVII") was in prison or, after his death (June 1795), the Comte de Provence as "Louis XVIII" remained a centre of Bourbon hopes and intrigues. The *émigré* nobles and clergy were nearly all royalist; so were some of the few who still remained at home or in hiding. The country people were monarchists at heart, with a cupboard-love republicanism. Federalism, as it was called, embraced the relics of the Girondin party, and members of all those classes which had suffered at the hands of the Jacobin government: hoarders, profiteers, dishonest officials, and those who were poorer owing to the depreciation of the currency or the redistribution of the land. The danger of foreign invasion had ceased; but the coastal blockade went on, and it would be a serious embarrassment to the Government if the armies were recalled from countries which they had "liberated", and upon which they lived, to become chargeable on the scanty supplies of the fatherland and to swell the numbers of its unemployed.

Robespierre had not been specially active in the execution of the Queen or of the Girondins; he had, indeed, protested against the indecent charges by Hébert which won sympathy for Marie-Antoinette, and though drafting the decree which closured the trial of the Girondin leaders, he had been content to imprison the seventy-three signatories of the protest against their arrest. He was ruthless in destruction, but discreet; he felt himself surrounded by intrigue, and had no wish to increase the number of his enemies. As for the war, his two speeches of November 17 and December 3, 1793, contain little more than denunciations of England and appeals to French patriotism. "The universe", he declared, "requires our survival", if only as a champion of the small states against the big tyrants. "The French Republic is as invincible as reason, as immortal as truth." "Patriotism triumphant, in spite of every vice that slavery taught us, and all the perfidy of our foes the people showing itself strenuous and prudent, formidable and fair, responding to the call of reason, learning to discern its enemies even under the mask of patriotism, and flocking to the colours to defend the magnificent fruit of its courage and virtue: such [he claims] is the expiation we offer to the world, whether for our own mistakes, or for the crimes of our foes." Fine words! But, reading between the lines, one can see that there were good political and economic reasons for encouraging the militant spirit of the country and for keeping the armies at the front. Yet a fresh danger was to arise from this policy. The Jacobinism of the troops, especially if their equipment and commissariat were mismanaged or their pay in arrears, might turn against the Jacobinism of politicians and a popular general with an army behind him might as easily become a menace as a support to the Government. Robespierre, who had long feared a military dictatorship, was the last person to overlook this danger.

But it was the common people, for whom the Jacobin regime had been planned and by whose aid it had come into being, and more particularly the common people of Paris, whom Jacobin centralisation was restoring to the supremacy which they had begun to lose under the decentralising tendencies of Girondism, from whom the greatest danger came. There could be no denying that the inhabitants of the poorer parts of Paris were suffering from unemployment, food-shortages, and rising prices: unemployment due to the emigration and the loss of foreign markets food-shortages due to the call-up of farm labourers and the civil war in the provinces and rising prices due to the depreciation of the *assignats*. How could people whose average wages were from 9½d. to 1s. 3d. a day afford milk at 6d. a pint, butter at 1s. 5d. to 2s. a pound, candles at 2s. 2d. a pound, soap at 3s. 5d., and tobacco at 3s. to 4s.? The Girondins, whose economic policy was *laissez-faire,* had done nothing to meet these grievances. When the Jacobins wanted popular support to overthrow them, they had backed the first *maximum* of May 1793. Now that they were in power they must do something to keep the city population quiet.

In the working-class sections of the east and south quarters of the city discontent was voiced and organised by the *Enragés* ("madmen"): Jean Varlet, a well-educated young agitator, Jacques Roux, a priest and a friend of Marat, Théophile Leclerc, and Claire Lacombe, an actress, who presided over a *société des femmes révolutionnaires* that Robespierre marked down for suppression in his little notebook. It was under pressure from these persons that, in June 1793, the Committee of Public Safety

sanctioned, unwillingly enough, the formation of the
armée révolutionnaire to requisition food for the capital,
and between July and September passed a law against
hoarding, a scheme for accumulating food-stocks in
greniers d'abondance (food-stores), and a revised *maximum*. But they disliked acting under compulsion they
wanted to do things in their own way, and to keep the
people beholden to the Government, not to the Opposition, for improvements in their condition. Barère and
Saint-Just had long-term schemes which would be com-
promised by half-measures. So, before the winter was
out, the *Enragé* leaders were in prison, the *femmes révolutionnaires* were suppressed, and the *armée révolutionnaire*, after being diverted to the siege of Lyon, was
disbanded. This would have been very well if the grievances of the poor had been due, as it was pretended, to
"Pitt's gold" and other foreign and counter-revolutionary
intrigues, and could be remedied by sending hoarders and
profiteers to the guillotine but, in fact, they were the
result of deep-seated economic troubles which the Jacobins did not understand and for which they had no ready
cure. The *Enragés* were dead, but *Enragisme* persisted
underground, and reinforced other forms of opposition
which, because they were political rather than economic,
held greater dangers.

One of these took the form of an exaggeration of Jacobin policy—always a difficult thing to check—in dealing
with the Church question. Ever since the enforcement of
the clerical oath under the Civil Constitution of 1790,
there had been non-juror clergy who escaped the penalties of imprisonment or deportation and carried on their
work in hiding in the remoter country parishes, particularly of the western departments. The Jacobin clubs and
Popular Societies tried to hunt them down, and were
soon assisted by emissaries from Paris; for there the
Commune was definitely anti-clerical, and the Convention had shown its hand by sanctioning clerical marriage
and instituting a Revolutionary Calendar in which *Décadi*
(every tenth day) took the place of Sunday, and the

Catholic saint's-days were absorbed into a new nomen-clature which attached to every day of the year the name of a domestic animal or an agricultural implement, a fruit or vegetable: the loss of holidays would be sweet-ened, it was supposed, by such incitements to labour. At Nevers, Fouché, a deputy, and Chaumette, a prominent member of the Paris Commune, conducted an anti-Catholic campaign which shocked local opinion. In the parish church of Vitry-sur-Seine, renamed a "Temple of Reason", a girl posed on the altar surrounded by busts of Voltaire, Rousseau, Marat, and Robespierre's friend the Jacobin martyr Le Peletier, with the singing of patri-otic hymns and a recitation of the Rights of Man. At Reims the deputy Rühl publicly broke in pieces the *sainte ampoule,* the flask of holy ointment used in the corona-tion of French kings. At Nancy the clergy renounced their Orders, and their licences were thrown on a ceremonial bonfire in the nave of the cathedral. Such excesses were not at all to the liking of the Jacobin government, which valued the support of the Catholic country-side and did not want a European reputation for atheism. Religious fanaticism, Robespierre declared, was no longer a serious danger. The Convention never intended to proscribe Catholic worship. "He who tries to stop the saying of Mass is a worse fanatic than the priest who says it." A decree was passed on December 6, 1793, reaffirming liberty of worship, and Chaumette perished as an atheist on the scaffold. But much damage had been done and many discontents remained behind.

Further harm was done to the Jacobin cause by a financial scandal in which some of its prominent members were implicated. The India Company (*Compagnie des Indes*), founded by Calonne and protected by Clavière, had been ruined by the blockade. Its liquidation fell into the hands of Fabre, a friend of Danton and Robespierre, and the author of the Revolutionary Calendar, with Basire, Chabot, and Julien, ex-members of the Committee of General Security, and Delaunay, a Jacobin deputy. These men conspired to make money out of the liquidation; and the plot, when discovered, was found (as usual in French *affaires*) to implicate a large number of more or less prominent Jacobins, as well as a group of alien Jews and foreign bankers. Some corrupt men (*pourris*) were to be found in every class; for everywhere there were men with new money to spend and temptations to invest it in *assignat* speculation, black-marketing, and other dishonest concerns. Danton himself, who had started his revolutionary career with a capital of £600, and whose second wife had brought him a dowry of £2,000, had been spending money at a far greater rate than these means allowed, and was commonly supposed to have received bribes from Montmorin and Mirabeau under the monarchy, and from the Spanish ambassador at the time of Louis' trial, in an effort to save the King. More recently he had been suspected of dealing too leniently with Dumouriez at the time of his treachery in the spring of 1793 and of having carried off wagon-loads of loot from Belgium. But he was still the hero of the Resistance in 1792, and a popular figure whom it would be dangerous to attack. Robespierre, to whom he was utterly antipathetic in tastes, temperament, and outlook, still counted him a colleague, if not a friend, and had written him a letter of condolence on the death of his first wife (February 1793), in which he described himself as "a warm and devoted friend", and said, "I love you more than ever, and I shall love you till I die". Danton himself, no longer a member of the Committee of Public Safety and sick of political life, had retired with his second wife (September 1793) to his country estate at Arcis, to enjoy, as he wished all men should do, the fruits of the Revolution. For the moment he was out of sight and out of mind.

Meanwhile the inquiries begun by the India Company affair transformed what might have been a financial scandal into a political plot. The *Enragés* were dead, the *pourris* were in prison, making accusations against one another, and the foreign bankers had discreetly retired beyond the frontier. But there remained a group of malcontents whose popularity or official position enabled them to voice the workers' demands for food, wages, and the Constitution of 1793. Their leaders were: Vincent, secretary for appointments under Bouchotte at the War Office; Ronsin, ex-commandant of the *armée révolutionnaire;* Momoro of the Cordeliers Club (the headquarters of the party); Carrier, the terrorist responsible for the *noyades* (wholesale drowning of prisoners) at Nantes, and some others. Their publicist was Hébert, *substitut-procureur* (deputy clerk) of the Commune, and editor of *Père Duchesne,* a low-class abusive Left-wing paper with the largest circulation in the country. The *Hébertistes,* as they were soon called, had no definite programme, but clamoured for popular control over military appointments, for a "purge" of the Civil Service, and for a strict use of the identity cards (*certificats de civisme*) issued by the *sections,* as a check upon political suspects. Again, these were not undesirable aims so much as interferences with the programme and work of the Committee—the Commune setting itself up in rivalry with the Convention: an informal and unparliamentary Opposition which might take advantage of a crisis, as the Jacobins themselves had done in 1793, to overthrow the Government. And always, at the back of such a movement, was the demand for the democratic Constitution of 1793, which the Jacobins had promised, but whose introduction would mean the dissolution both of the Convention and of the Committee. Thus the intensification of the Reign of Terror, which was the Government's reply to the Hèbertist challenge, was (as Engels wrote to Marx) "not the reign of people who inspire terror, but of people who are themselves terrified"—a judgment which might be passed on many other dictatorships.

It was not long before the Hèbertists gave the Government an opportunity for striking at them. They had fallen out with the Dantonists, the right wing of the Jacobin party, the men who thought the time had come for relaxing the regime of control and intimidation and for distributing the revolutionary bonus to citizen shareholders.

At the Cordeliers Club (March 4, 1794), it was resolved to drape the Declaration of Rights in mourning "until the people has recovered its sacred rights by the destruction of the faction" (i.e. the Dantonists); Vincent denounced "a conspiracy more formidable than Brissot's", and called for the use of the guillotine; Carrier announced a "holy insurrection"; and Hébert himself went so far as to denounce Desmoulins and to criticise Robespierre. Rumour said that there was a plot on foot to massacre the members of the Committee, if not the Convention, and to set up a Triumvirate of Hébert, Vincent, and Ronsin. The leaders were at once arrested; a political trial was staged in which the Hébertists were associated with offenders against the food laws and with dubious aliens; and on March 24 eighteen of these "conspirators" went to the guillotine. The only one not executed was a *mouton* (police spy) who had been put with them to report what they said in prison.

So much for the facts: what of the methods and motives? Let Robespierre speak for himself. On December 25, when the India Company affair was at its height, he had made a speech declaring that the Government was being attacked from two sides—by the extremists and by the reactionaries—and that, until the Republic had achieved liberty and peace, "the Government has to defend itself against all the factions which attack it; the punishment of the people's enemies [he added] is death". Robespierre had by now become an expert in conspiracies. His method was to construct from the speeches or publications of individuals or from the company they kept a common programme and policy, of which perhaps none of them was personally conscious, and to father it on them all. Thus when they were put on trial each found himself involved in vague charges, based on a casual word here, a conversation overheard there, or a piece of gossip started by some spiteful neighbour—charges which it was useless to disprove in detail, and which in their accumulated effect were fatal.

As for motives, those of the majority of the Committee

were undoubtedly public interest and personal fear; they had persuaded themselves that it was not the time for a change of government, and they were terrified lest, with Paris thinking otherwise, they might be forcibly overthrown and share the fate of their Girondin predecessors. But Robespierre, at least, looked farther. One has only to read his eloquent speech of February 5 on "the principles of political morality that ought to guide the National Convention" to see that the Reign of Terror was to him an ante-room to the Reign of Virtue. "What [he asks] is our aim? It is the peaceful enjoyment of liberty and equality, and the reign of that eternal justice whose laws are engraved, not on stone or marble, but in the heart of every man"; and by "every man" he means in effect the French people—"the first people in world-history to establish a real democracy, by inviting all men to share equality and the full rights of citizenship". The corollary of all this is *vertu:* virtue is the key-word of his philosophy. "Virtue is the natural quality of the people." In peace-time the Government might trust the people to be virtuous; but in a time of foreign and civil war it is necessary to "manage the people by argument, and the enemies of the people by intimidation". "If the basis of popular government in time of peace is virtue, its basis in time of revolution is both virtue and intimidation [*terreur*]—virtue without which intimidation is disastrous, and intimidation without which virtue has no power." So Robespierre tricked himself, as many idealists have done, into using bad means for good ends; only to find that means become ends, and that the thoroughfare is, after all, a *cul-de-sac.*

Soon after this speech Robespierre fell ill, and for some weeks was seldom seen at the Convention or the Club; but he reappeared at the meeting of the Committee on March 12, when the decision was taken to arrest the Hébertists. Between their arrest and trial he made several speeches denouncing the prisoners, and informing the public that, as soon as the Extremists had been dealt with, the Government would turn its attention to the Reactionaries. There was, in fact, no trial in our sense of the term, but merely an indictment of persons who must be guilty because the Government had decided that they were: the salaried judges and jury would give their assassination an appearance of legality, and the crowd could be trusted to applaud their execution. Such is the technique of dictatorship.

During the week following the execution of the Hébertists, the Committee perfected its plans for the elimination of the Dantonists. This was a more serious matter, for these "conspirators" included, besides Danton himself, Desmoulins, the originator of the attack on the Bastille, and the cleverest of the Jacobin journalists, Hérault de Séchelles, the author of the Constitution of 1793, and Fabre, the inventor of the Republican Calendar; sound party men, all of them, whose only crime was that they criticised the policy of their own government. In order to spread the responsibility for its action, and to give an added appearance of unanimity, the Committee of Public Safety called into counsel (as it had done once or twice before) the Committee of General Security; and the warrant for the arrest of the Dantonists, which can still be read, bore their eighteen signatures, scattered, as the custom was (the French equivalent of our "round robin"), over the breadth of the paper. Last but one, and smallest of all, comes the name "Robespierre". Certainly he must have hesitated to sign the death-warrant (for such it really was) of his old school-fellow, the friend to whom he had written a year ago, "I shall love you till I die". We have the evidence of Billaud-Varenne, whose signature heads the warrant, that Robespierre needed a deal of persuading before he added his name; and perhaps its niggardly insertion at the foot of the eighteen is some corrobation of this.

But it would be difficult to imagine him refusing to sign: it was part of his creed that no personal feelings should obstruct the duty of a patriot; and he was convinced that Danton, the hero of 1792, had become the traitor of 1794—that he had encouraged Fabre in his financial dishonesty and Desmoulins in his journalistic indiscretions, and that his name would head the list of the new Committee which the conspirators wished to substitute for the old. It is true that Danton's programme, according to the most trustworthy account, might seem innocuous enough: greater clemency towards political suspects, an amnesty for the expelled Girondin deputies, the introduction (in a revised form) of the Constitution of 1793, peace abroad, freedom of trade, and an end to the identity-card system. Did not the Committee itself profess just such aims? Yes, but as a long-term policy, to be carried out at its own time and in its own way; this attempt to undersell the Government in the market of national hopes was the most subtle and dangerous kind of Opposition; and to oppose the Government was to conspire against the nation. So the Dantonists must die.

So far it might be possible to excuse Robespierre's signature as forced out of him by party loyalty and a national emergency. But that is not the whole count against him. He had briefed his friend Saint-Just, who was chosen to present the case against the Dantonists, with a series of charges—against Fabre, against Desmoulins, and most of all against Danton—which show how far fear and fanaticism could go in distorting the judgment and corrupting the conscience of a moralist and idealist. In these notes, which unhappily for Robespierre's reputation have survived, Danton is accused of all kinds of actions and associations during the early years of the Revolution, which were innocent then but have now become criminal. It would be useless to examine them; all that mattered was their cumulative effect on the minds of jurymen and coffee-house politicians for whom the whole political Revolution previous to June 1793 could be written off (as it is by a school of modern historians) as a middle-class compromise (*bourgeois modérantisme*). This part of the charges was indeed common form in all the political trials of the period. More distinctive of Robespierre's point of view is the attempt to represent Danton's part in the national defence of 1792 as distracting the country from the dangers of foreign invasion; and his part in the retreat of the Prussians after Valmy as saving them from complete defeat. But the least creditable notes of all are those in which Robespierre allows his personal antipathy towards Danton to charge him with indulgence and immorality. He never (says Robespierre) attacked a real conspirator. He saved several persons from "the vengeance of the people" during the prison massacres. (This means Brissot and Roland, whom Robespierre had tried to involve in them.) He consorted with bad characters and tolerated vice. He once remarked that "the severity of our principles frightens people away from the patriotic party"; or again, "What do I care for public opinion? Public opinion is a whore, and it is nonsense to talk of posterity". Or, again, he would laugh at Robespierre's talk of *vertu,* and say, jokingly, that there was no sounder virtue than that which he practised every night with his wife. That Robespierre should have treasured up such trivialities, and used them to discredit his old friend, throws a strange light on that anæmic Puritanism of his, recoiling from the touch of the other's full-blooded vulgarity.

During the days before the trial, Robespierre kept the issue before the Club and worked up evidence against the prisoners. Some of them appealed to him for mercy— they could not realise how completely he had by now stifled his natural feelings—and got no answer. When the trial came on, the eloquence of Danton's defence was in danger of winning over the public and preventing the court from doing its duty. Fouquier-Tinville, the Public Prosecutor, appealed to the Committee. Saint-Just, alleging a prison plot to rescue the Dantonists, secured a decree from the Convention putting the defendants *hors des débats* (depriving them of the right of speech), and the scruples of the jury were overcome by submitting to them a secret document not produced in court. All but one of the accused men were condemned, and on April 6 fourteen of the most prominent Jacobins went to the guillotine, convicted of "a conspiracy aiming at the re-establishment of the monarchy and the destruction of the national representation and the republican government". There was no movement in the streets for the rescue of the popular heroes of 1789 and 1792. Only one protest had been heard in the Convention. Addresses were received from all over the country congratulating the Government on its heroic victory over yet another conspiracy. "Republican justice" was once more vindicated. The Reign of Terror would go on.

Chapter 8

A Republic of Virtue

THE TERROR would go on. Since public virtue could not be trusted to spring naturally from the soil of revolution, it must be forced. Robespierre was no apocalyptic visionary. He did not believe in letting the tares and the wheat grow together until the harvest. He believed it possible and necessary to root up the tares here and now; and he thought that he saw an end to the business, if revolutionary justice could avoid undue clemency on the one hand and undue severity on the other.

His idealism was confined to the people he did not know—the workers. His own class, the *bourgeoisie,* he viewed realistically. He had nothing of the bureaucrat's belief that committees, departments, and boards are above bribery or injustice. He had always held that the chief danger to the republic would come from its governing class, not from the masses. He disliked armies, because discipline made officers into bullies and *esprit de corps* enabled generals to become military dictators. He suspected every popular political leader of aiming at supreme power, and saw dictators everywhere—all the more so perhaps if he was fighting his own subconscious desire for dictatorship. What had excluded Marat from the Jacobin fellowship, and especially from Robespierre's circle, was not his sordid life or his bloodthirstiness, but his candid avowal that a dictator was needed and that he was ready to play the part. Dictatorship was the nightmare that beset the Jacobin bedside: the Revolution had begun as a great liberation from royal-feudal "tyranny"; its second act had been the abolition of the "despotic" monarchy; its third the overthrow of the Girondin bid for absolute control. It looked as though it would go full circle and end as it began.

Robespierre's draft for a "shadow" Constitution in 1793 had taken every precaution against this danger— partly by making every office accessible to the ordinary citizen, partly by providing popular checks on misgovernment. "The right of resisting oppression [said his Article 25] is a corollary of the other rights of men and citizens"; Article 27, "When a government violates the rights of the people, it becomes the most sacred duty of the whole people, and of each separate portion of it, to revolt against it"; and Article 28, "When a citizen can no longer rely upon the State to safeguard his rights, he falls back on his natural right to defend all his rights for himself". The final form of the Constitution of 1793, though in some points it fell below Robespierre's ideals, was in this respect even more plain-spoken. In a series of laconic Articles it declared that: "Sovereignty resides in the people: it is one and indivisible, imprescriptible and inalienable" (25). "No part of the people can exercise the power of the whole" (26). "Any individual who usurps the sovereignty may at once be put to death by free men" (27). "Public office is essentially temporary, and must not be considered as a distinction or a reward, but as a duty" (30). "Crimes committed by the people's representatives or agents must never go unpunished. No one has the right to claim more inviolability than other citizens" (31). "Resistance to oppression follows from the other rights of man" (33). And finally, in words even stronger than Robespierre's, "When the government violates the right of the people, insurrection is for the people, and for any part of it, the most sacred of its rights and the most indispensable of its duties" (35). A year later the decree constituting the Revolutionary Government, i.e. the Jacobin regime (December 4, 1793), contained not only an elaborate system for ensuring the efficient supervision of government and local officials, but also a section headed *De la pénalité des fonctionnaires publics et des autres agens de la République*, which enumerates in twelve Articles the penalties incurred for official offences; they range from deprivation of civic rights and confiscation of property to imprisonment in irons and death.

Nor can there be any doubt that Robespierre, whilst disliking the wholesale shooting of rebels, took a special interest in the discriminating execution of Government and local officials. It cannot have been by accident that, when the Committee of Public Safety, dissatisfied with the police work of the Committee of General Security, set up its own *bureau de police générale,* it entrusted its management to Robespierre and his special lieutenants Couthon and Saint-Just; or that this new department of justice concerned itself specially with official delinquencies. Its duties were "to supervise all the authorities and public agents co-operating with the administration, to exact a severe account from all such agents, and to prosecute any of them who shall be found taking part in plots, or perverting the powers entrusted to them against the cause of liberty". The *bureau* was installed, not very tactfully, in the same building as the Committee of General Security, which complained that "it was there that these Triumvirs [i.e. Robespierre, Couthon, and Saint-Just] drafted decrees in virtue of which persons whom we had released were arrested, and persons whose arrest we had ordered were set at liberty". The work was organised under sub-committees dealing with correspondence from different geographical areas and submitting daily reports to the head of the department; and a number of these reports still exist, with notes, mostly in Robespierre's hand: "Arrest him", "Send him to Paris" (i.e. to the Revolutionary Tribunal), and so forth. It is not known how many cases passed through the *bureau;* but it was an important purveyor of prisoners from the provinces to the capital, where it was now (since April 1794) the Government policy to concentrate all political trials.

So busy did the Revolutionary Tribunal become during 1793 that the single court which had done duty hitherto was sub-divided into two in August, and into four in September, with three vice-presidents, sixteen judges, and sixty jurymen; and the Public Prosecutor had five assistants. The forcible closure of the Hébertist and Girondin trials was not only a political expedient; it was also due to their holding up the routine work of the Tribunal. In the early summer of 1794 there were still between seven and eight thousand prisoners in Paris waiting to be tried; and more were arriving every day from the provinces, where perhaps ten times as many had been rounded up as suspects.

It was this situation which had suggested to Saint-Just his scheme of *Ventôse,* for subsidising the poor with the property of the prisoners. It was this which now suggested to Robespierre a more serious step. He remembered, though with disapproval of their application, the methods by which the rebels of Lyon and Marseille had been disposed of in batches of a hundred or so at a time. He had himself approved of the Commission set up under his friend Couthon at Orange, which in two months had condemned to death 332 out of 591 prisoners. This it had done by dispensing with the time-wasting formalities of witnesses and counsel. Why should not the Revolutionary Tribunal follow its example? Often in practice it had already done so, when counsel could not be found, and when the written evidence before the court, or the admissions of the prisoners, made witnesses superfluous. The *Law of the 22nd prairial* (June 10, 1794), after once more reorganising the Tribunal under four vice-presidents, twelve judges, and fifty jurymen, working in relays, declared that: "The Revolutionary Tribunal is instituted to punish the enemies of the people. The enemies of the people are all those who aim at destroying public liberty, either by force or by trickery." It then went on to instance eleven kinds of conduct that would fall under this general condemnation—drawn in terms so wide that hardly any suspect could escape the charge of treason (*anti-civisme*). Article 7 then laid it down that the only sentence the court could pass, in case of conviction, was death; and Article 8 that sufficient evidence for the death sentence could be found in "any kind of documents, material or moral, written or spoken, which naturally claim the assent of any just and reasonable mind"; explaining this vague account by adding that: "The standard of judgment [i.e. the decision as to what is good evidence] is the conscience of jurymen enlightened by patriotism: their aim is the triumph of the Republic and the ruin of its enemies." Finally, lest anyone might still suppose that the duty of the court was to *try,* and not merely to *convict,* Article 13 provided that if the jury thought it unnecessary to call witnesses, they could dispense with them; and Article 16 that patriotic jurymen were sufficient counsel for patriots wrongly accused, and that "as for conspirators, the law does not allow them to have counsel at all."

This Prairial Law, under which the number of cases heard was more than doubled, and the number of executions went up from 346 in May to 689 in June and 936 in July, has not unnaturally become notorious for its wholesale guillotining of persons deprived of any fair chance of defending themselves; and historical emphasis has been laid on the outstanding miscarriages of justices. But at the time this aspect was thought little of, compared with what might seem minor issues. The Committee of Public Safety were believed to approve of the policy embodied in the Prairial Law, and gave it their consent in principle; but they were not consulted again by Robespierre and Couthon before the final draft was submitted to the Convention. The other Committee, that of General Security, was not consulted at all. Suspicions were at once aroused, both in the Committees and in the Convention, that the law covered some intrigue on the part of Robespierre against the enemies of his party in the Assembly, and perhaps in the governing committees themselves. When the text was studied, it was found to contain an apparently harmless but possibly sinister provision: "The Convention [said Article 20] hereby does away with any provisions of previous laws inconsistent with the present decree." Was this as innocent as it looked; or was it intended to abolish the rule and custom of "parliamentary privilege", by which no deputy could be indicted before the courts without a specific vote of the

Convention? The Constitution of 1791, under which the deputies had been elected, and which was deemed to be still in existence until a new constitution was substituted for it, had declared that: "The national representatives are inviolable, and cannot be arrested, charged, or convicted for anything they may have said, written, or done in the exercise of their functions as representatives." This inviolability had been recognised in the very decree (April 1, 1794) which allowed the Assembly itself to overrule it. But in the proceedings against Danton, a few days later, he was put under "preventive arrest" first, and the Convention consulted afterwards—and the deputies were not likely to have forgotten it. Accordingly, they took the first opportunity (June 11) to pass a motion reasserting "the exclusive privilege of the National Representation to impeach and try its own members"; and, faced by this opposition, Robespierre and Couthon could do nothing but withdraw the obnoxious article and disclaim any sinister intentions. Nevertheless, the suspicion remained that the intention of the law had been not merely to speed up the Revolutionary Tribunal, but to direct its attention to a new class of suspects—the deputies themselves. The Robespierrists had too many enemies in the House to have any doubts as to the danger they might be incurring: if it was a slip, it was a serious one; if a challenge, they learnt that their bluff had been called.

There was one class of "traitors" whose punishment not only failed to improve the political situation but might even be said to make it worse. The schism in the French Church caused by the Civil Constitution and the penal laws against the non-juror clergy had added deep religious discontent to the other troubles of the countryside. The first of the penal laws, passed as long ago as November 29, 1791, began with a preamble (showing the nervousness of the Assembly) declaring that: "in dealing with the origin of these disorders it had listened to the universal assertion of all Frenchmen that the enemies of the Constitution had merely used religion as an instrument for troubling the earth in the name of heaven";

and went on to deprive non-juror clergy of their salaries, and to allow the local authorities to turn them out of their parishes or, if they were cantankerous, to imprison them for two years. Six months later another decree, due to the declaration of war (May 27, 1792), sentenced non-jurors to (voluntary) exile or (forced) deportation from the country, with an alternative of ten years' imprisonment. Three months later again, after the fall of the throne (August 26, 1792), yet another decree replaced imprisonment by deportation to Guiana. The previous decrees, like many passed by the Assemblies, had not been fully enforced; now some 25,000 priests fled the country, mostly to England. But some bishops and many clergy defied the decree, and remained, protected by their sympathisers. Robespierre himself had heard from his friend Lebon, a *curé* near Arras, how his non-juror predecessor was still making trouble in the parish.

The "de-christianising" campaign of 1793 was popular in the capital. But in the country parishes, especially of the west, the expulsion of a non-juror priest, partial or complete deprivation of Catholic sacraments, and the pulling down of the church bells (to be turned into coinage or gun metal) caused deep resentment, and contributed to the Girondist, "federal", and counter-revolutionary troubles of 1793–4. Whilst discontent amongst good Catholics had increased, the popularity of the patriotic cults of the early years of the Revolution had declined. Villagers no longer danced round the withered "Trees of Liberty"; baptisms and marriages at the "Altar of the Country" were no longer fashionable; the reading of the Rights of Man and the singing of the *Marseillaise* had become official functions and had lost their savour. *Décadi,* the tenth day, was the legal Sunday; but it would be only human nature to take a holiday on the seventh day too. Whilst anti-clerical deputies such as Fouché and Jacobin extremists such as Chaumette were exasperating popular feeling by their attacks on the Church, more sober representatives of the Government were asking for instructions. Mallarmé, for instance, on mission in the *Meuse et*

Moselle department, wrote to Robespierre in April 1794, saying that whilst officially the churches in that part of the country had been turned into Temples of Reason or Liberty, and the Communes had been ordered to hand over the church plate, the churches were still in fact open, Mass was being said, and services going on as usual. He asked the Convention to decide whether Catholic services can or cannot be openly held in "national buildings" that were once consecrated to Christian worship. What would the Government do?

The Committee of Public Safety had already, in November 1793, appealed to the Popular Societies, the local centres of Jacobinism, to use persuasion rather than violence in dealing with religious trouble. "Lay this truth to heart [they wrote], that consciences cannot be forced. Some people are honestly superstitious, and need encouragement to get rid of prejudices which others easily overcome. Frighten them, and they will withdraw. Sick souls like these must be encouraged to undertake a cure: to force it on them is to turn them into fanatics."

This letter was written in Robespierre's hand, and certainly represents his opinion. But how was persuasion to be brought to bear upon an ignorant and illiterate population, still at heart under the direction of the confessional, still devoted to the Mass? Could it perhaps be done by providing a genuine alternative to Catholicism; a Church embracing all good patriots, a creed to satisfy all men of good faith, and a ritual to rouse the enthusiasm of the crowd? That Robespierre had been feeling his way towards something of this kind is clear from parts of his speeches of November 21 and December 5, when he coupled religious toleration with the necessity of belief in the Supreme Being (*Etre Suprème*), an accepted philosophical (and indeed Catholic) term for God. He seems to have worked out his ideas during a three weeks' absence from the Convention after April 18: and it was on May 7 that he delivered his great speech in the Convention introducing the *Culte de l'Etre Suprème et de la Nature*. Like most of his set speeches, it is, to our minds, not a speech at all, but a lecture, at times almost a sermon, every sentence carefully studied, every effect calculated: with eloquence, certainly, but of a cold academic kind; unction, without real emotion; internal conviction that has no fellow-feeling for other men's beliefs. Yet it is the *apologia* of a fanatical patriot, the last testament of a republican idealist; and it is the most revealing document Robespierre has left to posterity.

He begins with a text from Rousseau: "Nature tells us that man was born for liberty; experience shows us man enslaved. His rights are written on his heart; history is the story of his humiliation." Rousseau was thinking in terms of political progress, as it is called. To Robespierre, as to the man of the twentieth century, the problem is the failure of morality to keep pace with science. "Everything is changed in the physical order; where is there any similar change in the moral and political order? The world has been half revolutionised: how can the other half be accomplished? Human reason is still like the globe it inhabits: half lit by the sun, and half shrouded in darkness." Why is this? Partly because man has not learnt to master his passions; partly because monarchical government has always been the enemy of enlightenment. France—the France of the Revolution—is two thousands years ahead of the rest of the world: "Yes, this charming land of ours, this pampered child of nature, was made to be the realm of liberty and happiness; its proud and sensitive people was born for glory and goodness. . . . I [he apostrophises his country], I am a Frenchman, thy representative. . . . Accept the sacrifice of my whole being! Blessed is the man who lives in thy midst! Thrice blessed he who can die for thy happiness!"

But even Jacobin France is not perfect yet. Much has been done in the past year; but much remains to be done. The bad old methods of monarchical government must be entirely reversed. "Immorality is the basis of despotism: the essence of Republicanism is virtue. The Revolution is the transition from the regime of crime to the regime of justice." Its progress has been delayed by enemies at home and abroad; and much of Robespierre's speech is taken up with denunciations of those corrupters of public morale—the Hébertists and their like—the secret agents of royalism and aristocracy, whom he vaguely classes together as "atheists".

What is the remedy? A fresh affirmation of religious belief: a national self-dedication of faith and service to the Divinity which (Robespierre had more than once asserted) directed the destiny of the Jacobin Republic.

"Think of nothing but the good of the country and the interests of humanity. Welcome every institution and doctrine that consoles and elevates the soul: reject any that tend to its degradation and corruption. . . . What saving grace is there in the arid doctrine of atheism? If you persuade a man that a blind fate presides over his destiny, and strikes down impartially the sinner and the saint; if you tell him that his soul is a mere breath that is dissipated at the door of death—what does it advantage him? . . . Will the idea of annihilation inspire purer and higher sentiments than that of immortality—more respect for himself and his neighbour, more patriotism, a braver resistance to tyranny, a truer devaluation of pleasure and of death?" Even if these ideas were no more than an illusion, they would be more useful than the so-called realities. "If the existence of God and the immortality of the soul were mere dreams, they would still be the finest creations of the spirit of man."

Upon this declaration of faith Robespierre builds his national church. "To the legislator [he declares], everything of practical use and value is true." None of the great law-givers of the past nationalised atheism; but they were all willing to make true religion attractive by embodying in it some elements of popular mythology: Lycurgus and Solon used the oracles, Socrates had his *daimon*. Frenchmen need not fear to be deceived, if they live in an age which has rediscovered the truths of natural religion: and there follows a discourse on the Encyclopædists, Rousseau, Condorcet, and other prophets of the God of Nature, the *Etre Suprème,* whose worship is to undermine both fanaticism and atheism, and unite all sectional faiths in the universal religion of Nature. The priests of the Catholic Church (he says) "created a God after their own image—jealous, capricious, greedy, cruel, implacable. . . . The true priest of the Supreme Being is Nature; his temple is the universe; his worship is virtue; his festivals are the rejoicings of a great people assembled under his gaze to renew the bonds of universal brotherhood, and to give him the homage of appreciative and pure hearts."

For the national church must have its creed, its festivals, its saints—the "heroic child" Bara, or Viala, who died for liberty at thirteen—and perhaps Robespierre himself will be its first martyr. . . .

In this high mood he proposes the fifteen Articles of the decree of May 7, 1794.

Article I.—The French people recognises the existence of the Supreme Being, and the immortality of the soul.

Article II.—It recognises that the proper worship of the Supreme Being consists in the practice of human duties.

Article III.—The most important of these duties are to hate treachery and tyranny, to punish tyrants and traitors, to succour the unfortunate, respect the weak and defend the oppressed, to do all the good one can to one's neighbour, and to treat no one unjustly.

Articles IV to VII enumerate the festivals designed "to remind men of the Deity, and of the dignity of their being": the anniversaries of July 14, 1789, August 10, 1792, January 21 and May 31, 1793, and the *décadist* "holy days" dedicated to "The Supreme Being and Nature", "The human race", "The French people", "The martyrs of liberty", "The republic", "Patriotism", "Truth", "Justice", "Stoicism", "Infancy", "Old age", "Misfortune", "Agriculture", "Our ancestors", and a dozen more apotheoses of political, social, and family virtues.

Articles VIII to X provide for the organisation of the new cult.

Article XI re-enacts the decree of 18 *frimaire* on liberty of worship; but Articles XII and XIII prohibit any "aristocratic" assembly or any likely to disturb the public peace, and provide severe penalties against religious agitators.

Finally, Articles XIV and XV provide for consequential orders, and fix a date a month ahead (20th *prairial*, June 8) for the first "National festival in honour of the Supreme Being".

It is on record that when Robespierre delivered his hanangue of May 7 his bearing had none of its usual nervousness; his tone was defiant; he knew that he was challenging opposition, committing himself and his party to an adventure of which the end could not be foreseen. There is reason to think that the introduction of the decree (whose preparation had been announced by his friend Couthon a month before) was held up by opposition on the Committee of Public Safety. Certainly, whilst the anticlericals of the Convention applauded the passages on fanaticism, and the respectable majority appreciated (though they may by now have been bored by) the attacks on the "atheists", there was little enthusiasm for the constructive proposals embodied in the decree. It was more acceptable to the atheists Maréchal and Lequinio, or the broad-minded Catholic Grégoire (who saw how under Article XI it could be exploited by the "constitutional" Church), than by the rank and file of the deputies, who, whether they were conventional Catholics or anticlericals, did not want the Republic to be tied up with any new-fangled religion, and did not believe that Frenchmen could be made virtuous "by Act of Parliament". Such support as the decree received came mainly from Jacobins of the Left, who thought that it would give the *coup de grâce* to the expiring Church, and from politicians who hoped that it would improve the reputation of the Republic in Protestant and even Catholic countries abroad.

Unhappily for the future of the measure, it came at a moment when tempers were high and suspicions deep, and during the month that elapsed between the promulgation of the decree and the first festival of the Supreme Being two incidents occurred which turned Robespierre's attempt to inaugurate his Republic of Virtue from a triumph into a defeat. On May 12 the Committee of General Security, the majority of whose members were anti-Robespierrists, ordered the arrest of a woman named Catherine Théot, a "prophetess' who was said to have written a letter proclaiming Robespierre's divine mission as a kind of emissary of the Supreme Being: her case did not become public for another six weeks; but it already gave rise to rumours and ribaldry at Robespierre's expense. On May 23 an attempt was made on the life of Collot d'Herbois by a man named Admiral; and it appeared that he had really intended to attack Robespierre. When, the next day, a girl named Cécile Renault tried to interview Robespierre at his lodgings, "to see what a tyrant looked like", and was found to have two knives upon her, it was natural to suspect that she was a second Charlotte Corday, and Maximilien was congratulated on having escaped the martyrdom he had foretold on May 7. The matter did not end there: the girl, her relations, and the supposed accomplices of both "assassins" were thrown into prison; it was evident that another "plot" had been discovered, and that another mass execution was being prepared; but this time not for political enemies of the Revolution, but for personal enemies of Robespierre.

On June 4 Robespierre was elected by an almost unanimous vote President of the Convention, and on June 8 he presided over the flamboyant ceremonies designed in honour of the Supreme Being by David, the official pageant-master of the Revolution. First, in the Tuileries gardens, he delivered two orations and set fire to an effigy of Atheism, out of whose ashes rose an image of Wisdom; then he headed a procession to the Champ de Mars (renamed *Champ de la Réunion*), dressed in blue, with one bouquet at his breast and another in his hand; and there sat on an artificial "Mountain" under a "Tree of Liberty", whilst a hymn was sung to the Supreme Being, swords flourished, and guns fired, amidst cries of *Vive la République!* and universal rejoicings. He was proud of his position: it was the greatest day of his life; but he could hardly fail—for he was the most suspicious man alive—to notice the jealous looks that followed him or to overhear the sarcastic remarks of his enemies.

Nothing is more difficult for the historian than to discover the general trend of public opinion in an age and country that had no clear means of expressing it—no popular or impartial press, no "mass observation", no novels of common life. He cannot judge the state of mind in a provincial town from the addresses sent in to a Jacobin government from the local Jacobin Club; or the opinions of the peasantry from—what, indeed, but the inarticulate "passive resistance" of the country-side in face of any sort of innovation? In the more important centres of Jacobinism the first Article of Robespierre's decree might be inscribed on the churches, and the observance of *décadi* instead of Sunday (obligatory for officials by the law of December 8) be made a test of patriotism and an opportunity of popularising the new cult. In places where Catholicism was still strong, the *Etre Suprême* was sanctified, as pagan and patriotic cults had been, by being associated with the *Veni Creator* and the Mass—all the more easily as June 8, 1794, was Whit-Sunday. But in most parts of the country the rites of the new religion were ignorantly confused with those of the old—the "Tree of liberty", the "Altar of the country", the "Eye of vigilance", and the *"Marseillaise"; the* common people looked on without interest whilst the *municipalité* went through the dull routine of *décadisme;* and within a few months the *Culte de l'Etre Suprême* was as dead as any other attempt to extemporise an alternative to an ancestral worship, an ingrained superstition. Robespierre's dream of a State religion which would unite all men of good will in the worship of the God of them all, and in the practice of the social and domestic virtues, died with him; or perhaps with the old Jacobin, Renan's friend, who treasured to the end of his life the faded nosegay tied with a tricolor ribbon which he had carried on June 8, 1794.

Chapter 9

The Fall of Robespierre

WHEN THE SUNNY DAYS of June 1794 were followed by the sweltering heat of July—always a dangerous season in Paris—it became obvious that another political crisis was at hand. Even if no special occasion should precipitate its fall, there were good reasons to foresee that the Jacobin government would not outlive by much more than a year the Girondin regime which it had overthrown in June 1793. What were the grounds of this expectation?

It was a provisional government, set up to deal with a national emergency—the complicated crisis of the spring of 1793. Its leaders in the Convention, and its agents in the Paris Commune, the Jacobin clubs, and the Popular Societies had gradually ousted their Girondin rivals from every position of power. This process had been helped by the promise of an exceedingly democratic constitution. But when the Girondin leaders had been liquidated, the constitution was indefinitely postponed, "until the peace", and the government of the country fell into the hands of a Standing Committee of the Convention; "government" meaning the initiative in legislation, direct control of the Executive and Administration, the direction of the armed forces and police, and the power of life and death exercised through a Tribunal that was above the law. France and Paris might tolerate this dictatorship of a committee so long as the emergency that gave rise to it still existed; so long as there was danger of foreign invasion or of counter-revolution at home; so long as the victims of the guillotine were priests, aristocrats, or dishonest contractors; and so long as tradesmen could make their profits, artisans earn decent wages, and housewives be sure of food and clothing at reasonable prices. But were these conditions being any longer fulfilled in the summer of 1794? And if not, what was the remedy? The Constitution of 1793, followed by a general election, a new National Assembly, and a renewal of the old struggle between rival parties? Or a popular (or rather Parisian) rising against the Jacobin monopoly of power? Or a *coup d'état* by the Robespierrists which would leave the Government in the hands perhaps of a triumvirate, perhaps of a dictator? In this state of uncertainty everything depended on certain points of weakness in the Jacobin government.

A minority government is not necessarily an unrepresentative one. What does representation mean, if not that the majority delegate the business of government to a minority, whether King and Ministers, or members of Parliament, or a civil bureaucracy? So long as the Governing Committee of 1793 represented the Convention and the Convention represented the nation, minority government need carry no stigma. Trouble only arose because there was no constitutional provision (as, for instance, by-elections) for altering the personnel of the Convention, or forcing a general election, or carrying through a change of government. Such changes had come about in 1789 by the summoning, under popular pressure, of a National Assembly that no one had heard of for 175 years: in 1791 through the first written constitution that France had ever had; in 1792 by the forcible overthrow of the monarchy; and in 1793 by a *coup d'état,* in which the "Opposition", helped by the people of Paris, proscribed and guillotined the leaders of the "Government". Probably no constitution, in the sense of an overruling "law and custom", could have been constructed and observed in a country which had never had one; certainly not during a time of social revolution and foreign and civil war. But the desire for it remained, if only in the negative form of unhappy memories of the arbitrary government of pre-revolutionary days. The Constitution of 1793, which the Jacobins had held out as a bait to catch anti-Girondin voters, and then set aside, remained as a constant reproach to their single-party dictatorship, and was the one operative article in the programmes of successive "factions"—*Enragés, Hébertistes, Dantonistes.*

The Jacobins, having taken the *sansculottes* of Paris into their pay to overthrow the Girondins, were now the victims of a political blackmail, and found that they must try to buy off the people by *panem et circenses*—find them food and employment, punish their oppressors, and tolerate the violences of the Commune. But they soon found that concessions earned, instead of gratitude, fresh demands; and they were driven into punitive measures— the suppression of the *armée révolutionnaire,* a *maximum* of wages, the arrest and execution of food-hoarders, the liquidation of agitators and demagogues. Every such step extended the area of public discontent. Though it is a mistake to suppose that during the Reign of Terror ordinary Parisians feared for their lives or lay awake at night expecting to hear the police beat on the door and hurry them off to prison, yet it must be remembered that each individual who lay in prison or suffered on the guillotine created a group of enemies of the Government: if one assumes an average of three children to a family and three generations living the number of relations affected by each arrest would be seventy, not to mention friends of the family. With a total of 1,832 executions in Paris alone up to the end of June 1794 (though not all were Parisians), no one knows how many in the provinces, and many thousands of prisoners, discontent became formidable, especially amongst the many who belonged to what were called the *queues* (followers) of Hébert, Danton, and other proscribed leaders; men doubly bitter against the Government and only waiting for an opportunity to have their revenge.

Some historians attach special importance to the view that, with the victory of Fleurus (June 26), all serious danger on the frontiers was at an end, that there was no longer any reason for an Emergency government, and that a popular demand was heard for a return to normal conditions. In fact, Fleurus came too late to affect the situation; it was not victory the country wanted, but peace; and there was no corresponding cessation of hostilities on the home front, which the Robespierrists always regarded as the more serious danger. For it was true—and remained so for some years—that, whilst Frenchwomen wanted their husbands and sons home again, their return would have meant an economic readjustment which the Government had no wish to face, and this added another stress to an already overweighted structure.

In provincial towns where Catholicism was strong, and, generally speaking, in the country districts where non-juror clergy might still be found, religion was the Government's most subtle and pervasive enemy. Every village without a priest, every church without Mass, every death without Christian burial, was an argument against Jacobinism. The National Assembly, the legatee of the Most Catholic Kingship, had failed either to co-operate with the Papacy or to supplant it. The country waited desperately for a new Concordat. These religious troubles were not specially the fault of the Jacobins, who had maintained freedom of worship, at least in theory, and had tried to suppress the "de-christianisers". But who was there to blame—who is there ever to blame—except the Government of the day? It was the same with the complicated economic ills from which the country was suffering—inflation, food-shortage, the blockade: they were not due to the Jacobins, who had inherited them from the Girondins and had at least tried to remedy them, but to what would now be called a "world situation", and to secondary causes for which the political economists of the time knew no cure. Indeed, their ultimate reason was war, the mother of all ills: war that the Girondins had begun in order to put themselves in power, and that the Jacobins would end, if they could do so without putting themselves out of power.

Nevertheless, in spite of labour troubles in the industrial centres and religious troubles in the countryside, the Jacobin government was less afraid of the people than of the politicians. The "Third Estate", which had made and directed the Revolution, was still, for all effective purposes, the *bourgeoisie;* the proletariat, the workers, the "Fourth Estate" as it was sometimes called, remained illiterate, unorganized, politically voiceless; their protests could only take the shape of food-riots, noisy demonstrations, and occasional lynchings. The real danger, for a single-party dictatorship, came from possible rival parties—the "factions" secretly organised against the "patriots"—*Enragés, Hébertistes, Dantonistes:* each in turn was destroyed, but out of its ruin new factions arose; it is a common experience. Now there was added to these enemies a fresh party of opposition created within Jacobinism itself by fear and hatred: fear of an extension of the Jacobin "purge" to persons hitherto exempt—the new "privileged" class to which the Revolution had given birth; and hatred of the Robespierrist predominance and policy. The *Law of the 22nd prairial,* prepared by Robespierre, and Couthon before the "Fête of the Supreme Being", and brought to the Convention only two days after it, showed not merely that Robespierre's religious programme was that of a Calvin—Paris to be a second Geneva and no mercy to be shown to a political Servetus—but also that deputies would no longer be covered by parliamentary privilege, but were as much at the mercy of the Committee, the Public Prosecutor, and the Tribunal as any non-juror priest or *émigré* aristocrat. This part of the design had failed; but the deputies remembered the fate of Danton, and those of them who suspected that they were on Robespierre's black list—Fouché for his anti-Catholic and terrorist extravagances, Vadier for taking up the Théot case, Tallien for his conduct at Bordeaux, Dubois-Crancé and Ysabeau at Marseille, a group who afterwards admitted that they had been plotting for his overthrow, and many more whose dislike of Robespierre was concealed by fear—none of these would need much persuasion to join in a conspiracy against the Government.

But there was no need to use violence. The Convention could, if it wished, get rid of the whole Committee of Public Safety, or of any part of it, constitutionally, either by refusing its re-election or by sanctioning the arrest of any of its members. Of the two methods, Robespierre's enemies preferred the second; for they wished him permanently out of their way. Accordingly these men set themselves to work on the feelings of the deputies, and to stage an attack upon the Robespierrists in the Convention which should end in a decree for their arrest and trial. It may be objected, had not the Jacobins a working majority in the Convention and would they not defeat any such attempt? A few months earlier this might have been so; but not since the decree of May 7, and the law of June 10; nor was it ever safe to prophesy how the real majority of the Assembly, the non-party members of the "Marsh," would vote in a crisis. Robespierre's domineering manner might alienate them at the last minute; clever management of the debate might decide the issue.

Even so, it might still be useless to attempt anything if the Government stood firm and united and defied the Convention, relying on the support of the Jacobin Club and the Commune. But this was just what they could not do. The Government was divided, member against member, committee against committee: the Club might fall in behind its most popular speaker, but the Commune could do nothing without the consent of its constituent *sections* and the support of their battalions of the National Guard; and no one knew what line the *sections* would take in a contest between the Convention and the Commune.

"Member against member." It had been obvious from the first that the Committee of Public Safety, though held to their desks by their departmental duties and to their daily conference by the necessity of a common policy, were by no means a happy family. Robespierre, Couthon, and Saint-Just were the theorists and policy-makers of the Committee; and the frequent absences of the two last made it, in effect, a party of one—one who in any case stood out from the Committee by his experience, his intransigence, his influence on the Club, and his pulpit eloquence, as the figure-head of the Jacobin party. The executive members of the Committee, as they might be called—Carnot, Lindet, Saint-André, and the two Prieurs —accepted this policy, but were too busy to pay much attention to it; whilst as professionals they resented the interference of men they regarded as amateurs: Carnot had quarrelled with Saint-Just about the Dutch campaign, and his army paper, *La Soirée du Camp,* was definitely anti-Robespierrist. Billaud and Collot were openly hostile to the Robespierrist clique and ready to join in any attempt to get rid of them. Billaud resented Robespierre's domineering tone and virtuous poses and had attacked the "modern Pericles." Collot did not forget that he had nearly been assassinated by mistake for Robespierre, and had hinted, like Billaud, that it was time to get rid of the "tyrant." Some of the "professionals" agreed with them in disliking the *bureau de police,* the *Culte de l'Etre Suprème,* the Prairial Law, and the Laws of Ventôse. They had all accepted, and were collectively responsible for, the Reign of Terror: no suspect went to the guillotine without the sanction of the Committee. But they regarded it as a necessary means to the end of victory abroad and discipline on the Home Front: they had no sympathy with its use as a method of enforcing Robespierre's moral reformation or Saint-Just's redistribution of property. Accordingly, when it came to an attack upon the Robespierrist triumvirate, they would not unite against the Convention. They were tired of all these quarrels, and would not be sorry if they could purchase their own immunity by the sacrifice of three troublesome colleagues.

The only member of the Committee whose temperament, long service, and willingness to become "all things to all men" fitted him to reconcile these difference was Barère,—Barère, who had made himself not merely indispensable to the Government but also popular with the Paris crowd, which cheered his rousing speeches (*carmagnoles*) in honour of republican victories, and nicknamed him "the Anacreon of the guillotine." It was Barère who made a last attempt to reconcile the Robespierrists to the Committee by proposing that it should implement Saint-Just's Laws of Ventôse, which had hitherto remained a paper programme. This seems to have been the agenda for a joint meeting of the two Committees on July 23. For the Committee of General Security had more than once recently been called into conference with that of Public Safety, though all its members were known to resent the *bureau de police* and some of them were declared anti-Robespierrists; no doubt the "political" committee did this deliberately in order to associate the "police" committee with their policy and to disarm its opposition. At this meeting Robespierre refused Barère's olive-branch, and put himself in the wrong by attacking by name opponents who already suspected that they were on his next list for proscription. The official account of the meeting said that the Government was united; probably nobody believed it. So the stage was set for the last act of the drama.

It might seem by this time that Robespierre was courting the martyrdom that he had foretold. It was hardly necessary for the malcontents to name any enemy except himself. Ever since the middle of April one stroke of aggression and challenge had followed another: on April 16, within ten days of the execution of Danton, the *bureau de police,* with its inquisition into the conduct of Government agents and civil servants; on May 7 the decree inaugurating the new religion; on June 8 the "Fête of the Supreme Being"; two days later the Law of the *22nd prairial;* and within a week the wholesale execution—perhaps the most abominable of the series—of fifty-eight persons supposed to be implicated in the attack on Robespierre on May 24, all wearing the red shirts (*chemises rouges*) of parricides—for had they not tried to murder the "father of the country"? Was it surprising if the Paris tradesmen and artisans, the moderate members of the Convention and Commune, and those of Robespierre's colleagues whom he took little pains to conciliate grew alarmed and talked of "dictatorship"?

What was he really thinking of? It was not easy then, and it is not easy now, to read his mind. He penned no apologia. No letter in his hand survives later than an urgent summons to Saint-Just in the name of the Committee, to return to Paris to deal with "new dangers" and a "revival of factions more alarming than ever," written on May 24, the day of Cécile Renault's supposed attack upon his life. There can be no doubt that his courage was all moral: physically he was a coward; the *chemises rouges* execution was a measure of the fear which haunted him for the rest of his days. It was not lessened by evidence of other and perhaps more serious plots: the *affaires* Lecointre, Marcandier, Rouvière, Legray. The guillotine seemed to breed new victims. Never was the foolish boast of the terrorist—*les morts ne reviennent pas* ("the dead are done for")—so disproved. Did Robespierre suspect this? Did he begin to distrust his own principle that virtue was powerless without intimidation? Was he looking for a way to adapt to his own ends the policy of clemency for which he had condemned the Dantonists? Was he, at least, a victim of that fatal delusion of terrorists that just one more purge will clear the way for a general amnesty; that only one obstacle still stands between an apparent *impasse* and an open Paradise?

At any rate, for more than a month from the third week in June he almost disappeared from public life, making no speeches in the Convention between June 18 (when his fortnight as President ended) and July 26, and only two at the Club between June 11 and July 9, and apparently attending the Committee only on two or three occasions; after June 30 he even gave up his work at the *bureau de police*. He must have known—he remembered the case of Danton—how dangerous it might be to fall out of public attention and to leave the political field free to his enemies. It is reasonable to suppose that he wanted leisure to think out his position and to plan his next step, in view of growing opposition. He may have counted on his opponents falling out amongst themselves and on his being able to come forward again as the one man with a clear policy that would save the State. He may have been making up his mind for a desperate throw—a final appeal to the "patriots" and the "people," with an "all or nothing" alternative, dictatorship or martyrdom. He had been urged by his friend Payan on June 26 to take up the challenge thrown down by the Committee of General Security in the Théot affair by presenting another *grand rapport* like that of May 9, attacking "the conspirators," and using all the official means at the disposal of the Government "to centralise and standardise public opinion or in other words to set up a moral Control equivalent to the physical and material Control" already exercised by the Jacobin government. That was no doubt what he would have liked; but could it be done? His refusal of Barère's olive-branch on July 23 seems to show that he reckoned he could not count on the support of the Committees, and was determined to appeal over their heads to the Convention and the People.

This intransigence offended even his friends Couthon and Saint-Just. Couthon on June 24 admitted that there were personal differences within the Committee; Saint-Just prepared a speech for the Convention which was to contain his own Ventôse plan, but to be silent about Robespierre's *Etre Suprème*. Robespierre himself knew what he was going to say, and was reported by a friend to be well aware of his dangerous position but ready to risk his life in a last attack on the conspirators. They, for their part, spent the time preparing the ground in the Convention. Fortunately for their purposes, Collot was now President, and could be trusted to favour the Opposition: it was arranged beforehand who would head the attack and how the arrest of the Robespierrists should be carried through.

The attack was timed for July 27 (9th Thermidor). At the previous meeting of the Convention, on the 26th, Robespierre was to have his say: his enemies calculated that, as things were, this would win them fresh votes. The speech which he delivered that day was his final challenge to his enemies, the fullest exposition of his revolutionary creed, his only apologia, his "last will and testament." It exists only in a text printed after his death from a rough copy found amongst his papers; but there is no reason to doubt that this version is sufficiently accurate.

He begins with an uncompromising claim to be speaking "useful truths"; to be defending the authority of the Convention and his own innocence against the attacks of "tyrants." The French Revolution, "the first ever based on the rights of man and the principles of justice," has been corrupted by a series of conspiracies, and the life of the Republic is in danger—the life of the very Convention, and of himself too, its champion against traitors and conspirators, its defender from immorality and atheism. The opponents of the Government can hardly reproach it with too much severity towards such traitors as Hébert, Ronsin, Chabot, Danton, Fabre, and Lacroix; but now they are going about saying that new proscription lists are being prepared by the Committee, by himself. Well—Robespierre grasps the nettle—why not? Why not, if in the name of the country, and to destroy factions that threaten its safety? Why not, so long as there is no question of a dictatorship—and this charge he indignantly rejects? Why not, in the cause of Virtue, "that tender, imperious, irresistible passion, at once the torment and delight of magnanimous minds, that profound hatred of tyranny, that compassionate zeal for the oppressed, that sacred love of one's country, that still holier and more sublime love of humanity?" Hébert and Danton are dead, but Hébertism and Dantonism still survive, in the "indulgence" which would impede the work of the *bureau* and the *tribunal,* and in the "atheism" which obstructs the cult of morality and religion.

At last Robespierre comes to the practical proposals which his audience impatiently waited for. It is the Government itself, he declares, which needs purging. "We must not slander it, but we must recall it to its first duties, simplify it, reduce the number of its agents." Most of its members are sound men; but they are embarrassed by a small number of traitors, who disorder the national finances and carry punitive measures to excess. Here, for the first time, if the report is to be trusted, he mentioned names—"men like Cambon, Mallarmé, and Ramel," with special stress on Cambon. And he ended with proposals which could have left no doubt that other individuals, too, were in danger: "to punish the traitors; to appoint new members to the Sub-Committees of the Committee of General Security; to purge this Committee itself, and put it under the Committee of Public Safety; to purge that Committee, too, and reestablish a centralised government [*constituer l'unité de gouvernement*] under the supreme authority of the National Convention, its centre and its supreme court of appeal."

So he had burnt his boats, he had staked all on one throw, he had declared war on his own colleagues; and his enemies must have rubbed their hands at his last words: "If it is impossible to propose these measures without being charged with personal ambition, I can only conclude that they are anathema, and that we are under a reign of tyranny: not that I must hold my peace. What answer is there to a man who is in the right and who is not afraid to die for his country?"

The reception of Robespierre's proposals was sufficiently ominous. Attempts were made to draw him into further personalities; and it was proposed that, instead of the official printing of the speech—the almost meaningless compliment that every important orator expected—it should be referred to the Committees "for examination." Robespierre might console himself by reading it again to the Jacobin Club the same evening; but even there his right to speak was disputed by Collot and Billaud, and Javogues interrupted his opening words with the cry, "We want no dictators here!" When he came to the end, he added a new peroration, more suitable for a society in which he had so many friends. "The speech which you have just heard [he is reported as saying] is my last will and testament. My enemies are so many and powerful that I cannot long hope to escape their blows. Never have I felt so much emotion in addressing you: for I fancy that I am saying farewell. Whatever may happen, my memory will always be revered in your virtuous hearts. That is enough for me. But the Republic [he went on] needs something more." And he proceeded to incite them to defy the Convention and to destroy the traitors. But perhaps he expected no response. "If you support me [he ended], the new traitors will share the fate of the old. If you forsake me, you will see how calmly I shall drink the hemlock." David was so moved by the way he spoke these words that he exclaimed, "I will drink it with you!" But he never did. Nor did the Club do anything next day beyond declaring itself in permanent session and passing a resolution affirming its intention "to conquer or to die."

The big echoing *Salle des machines* in the Tuileries was more crowded than it had been for many weeks when the deputies moved into their semicircle of seats on July 27. For so long there had been nothing to do but listen to Government reports and vote in favour of Government decrees. Today it was different. Something was at last going to happen, and no one knew how things might go. Sain-Just's report on behalf of the Committee was the first item on the agenda. His cool uncompromising intelligence had been employed before now to give point to the denunciation of some conspiracy. Would it be the same today? Did the choice of Robespierre's young admirer mean that the Committee had once more surrendered to Robespierre's dictation; or was the rumour true that Saint-Just had broken with his master, and might even denounce him? He was not allowed to explain; for he had only spoken a few words when Tallien, no doubt by previous arrangement, interrupted him, declaring that Robespierre and his friends were no more than another of the factions they were so fond of denouncing, and that they were destroying the unity of the country. Then Billaud jumped up and joined in the denunciation, calling Robespierre a dictator. When Robespierre tried to make his way to the tribune, which stood opposite the deputies' semicircle of seats, there were prearranged cries of "Down with the tyrant!" Tallien declared that he had brought a dagger to plunge into his heart. On his motion and Billaud's the House voted the arrest of the Robespierrist Hanriot and his officers, who might yet (as they had done a year ago) lead the National Guard against the Convention.

When Robespierre made another attempt to speak, there were cries for Barère. It would have been characteristic enough of that "Trimmer" if, as has been said, he had brought two speeches in his pocket, one in favour of Robespierre and one against; in fact, he seems to have dealt with the dangers of a military or royalist *coup d'état,* a quite irrelevant warning. He was followed by Vadier of the Committee of General Security, with a long list of grievances against Robespierre, especially the Théot affair, which was his speciality. Tallien again took up one of his points. At last Robespierre reached the tribune, and addressed himself in despair to the Moderate deputies of the Centre—"for you are honest men, not brigands." Once more shouted down, he appealed to the President for the right to be heard. His voice was too weak to overbear the interruptions. "It's Danton's blood that's choking him," sneered Garnier. His retort, "Is it Danton, then, that you are avenging?" was the last thing he was heard to say. Louchet proposed his arrest. Amid cries of "Vote!", young Augustin Robespierre, whose chief virtue was brotherly affection, claimed to be included in the decree, as did his friend Le Bas, of the Committee of General Security. So it was put to the House, and carried unanimously, with cries of *Vive la Liberté!* and *Vive la République!* Robespierre was taken to the bar of the House, and there, along with his brother, Saint-Just, Couthon, and Le Bas, placed under arrest.

This was not necessarily the end. True, arrest meant trial, and what chance had Robespierre, under his own Prairial Law, of a fair hearing, or of any sentence but that of death? But there was still the possibility of an appeal to the Commune, of a rescue by Hanriot's National Guardsmen, and of an armed rising against the Convention. The Assembly had tried to scotch any action on the part of the Commune by its decree against Hanriot, and by summoning the Mayor and Town Clerk, both prominent Robespierrists, to the Assembly; but Hanriot had not been arrested, and Lescot-Fleuriot and Payan, remembering August 10, had refused to come. Indeed, when they heard of Robespierre's arrest, these officials summoned a special meeting of the *conseil-général* of the Commune, and immediate steps were taken—the sounding of the tocsin, the closing of the city gates, the mobilising of the Guard—which amounted to armed insurrection against the Government. But whether it would be effective depended on the attitude of the *sections:* 21 out of the 48 made no move; 27 waited to see what would happen, and some of them ultimately declared for the Convention, but only 13 sent their battalions of the Guard to defend the Town Hall against a possible attack by the Convention. The governors of the Paris prisons, who were responsible to the Commune, were instructed not to receive the arrested Robespierrists, and they ultimately found their way to the Town Hall, where a special Executive Committee sat all night to deal with any emergency. The Convention, which had adjourned at 5:30, met again at seven o'clock, to be faced with the news of the escape of their prisoners and of the defiance of the Commune. Some hours were wasted in futile debate, but at last the bold step was taken—the only one fit for the situation—of declaring the Robespierrists outlawed (*hors la loi*), so that they and any who helped them could be arrested and executed without trial; and Barras, a deputy with some military experience, was put in command of whatever troops might be available to carry out this decision.

In the middle of the night, after the escaped Robespierrists had arrived at the Town Hall, the Executive Committee retaliated against the decree of outlawry by issuing warrants for the arrest of the leading anti-Robespierrists, and by summoning the *sections* to come to their aid; a special letter sent to Robespierre's own *section des Piques* may still be seen in the Carnavalet Museum, and at its foot the two first letters, *Ro,* of his tiny signature. But the *sections* did not respond; and the few Guardsmen who were already on parade in the Place de Grève gradually dispersed. When at two o'clock in the morning of the 28th Barras and his men arrived at the Town Hall, they entered unopposed, and broke into the room where the

Committee was still sitting. Saint-Just let himself be arrested without a struggle. Augustin Robespierre, Couthon, and Hanriot tried to escape by windows or stairs, and were picked up injured outside. Le Bas had a pair of pistols; with one he blew out his brains; with the other Robespierre tried to shoot himself, but only shattered his jaw. He was carried through the streets on an improvised stretcher to the Tuileries, and laid on a table in the ante-room of the Committee of Public Safety. There he remained for the rest of the night. A surgeon dressed his wound. Early next day he was transferred to the Conciergerie prison, and thence brought before the Revolutionary Tribunal, not for trial but for formal identification. At six o'clock in the morning he was taken in a cart along the rue Saint-Hororé, past the *manège,* past the Jacobin Club, past his empty lodgings at the Duplays, to the place de la Concorde, and there his head was struck off by the guillotine.

It was six weeks since he had passed by the same route at the head of the Convention, in the procession in honour of the *Etre Suprème:* the same crowd was here today; but its cries were *A bas le tyran! A bas le maximum!* The Jacobin rule, the Jacobin programme had been rejected. The only patriot who believed in the people, and might have refounded the French Republic on virtue and religion, had been put to death by his fellow-citizens, in accordance with Article 17 of his own constitution: *Que tout individu qui usurperoit la souveraineté, soit à l'instant mis à mort par les hommes libres.*

Chapter 10

Robespierre

So ROBESPIERRE DIED; and for forty years, under the last days of the Convention, the Directory, the Consulate and Empire, and the Bourbon restoration, his memory was burdened with all the crimes of the Revolution. Only when the *bourgeois* monarchy of Louis-Philippe reiterated that of Louis XVI under the Constitution of 1791, and seemed likely to end in the same way, was it profitable and *à propos* to investigate the career of the men who had guided the destinies of the first French republic, and typified Jacobinism at its best and at its worst. Since the publication of Buchez and Roux's *Histoire parlementaire de la Révolution française* in 1834–8, it has been impossible to remain content with the simple verdict of "guilty" passed by the victims and victors of Jacobinism. There followed two books of lasting influence, Lamartine's romantic *Histoire des Girondins* and Louis Blanc's massive *Histoire de la Révolution française,* both of which culminated in Robespierre and Robespierrism. The revolutionists of 1848 issued a paper called *Robespierre,* in which many of the catchwords of the Revolution of 1793 reappeared, and articles purporting to be signed by the Jacobin martyrs of 1793–4 incited Parisians of another age to emulate their deeds. Michelet, perhaps, in his great national history, was the first Frenchman to honour Robespierre as a democrat and to condemn him as a terrorist.

And this was the English view, foreshadowed by the way in which such sympathisers with the early revolution as Wordsworth and Arthur Young changed their minds under the influence of the execution of the King, the Reign of Terror, and the war of 1793. Croker, who had collected numerous pamphlets and opinions in Paris, was puzzled by Robespierre, and inclined to believe that "the chief cause of his fall was his being suspected of an intention of returning to some system of decency, mercy, and religion". Carlyle's "sea-green Incorruptible" was a figment of his brilliant imagination, truer than life, and has, with Dickens' *Tale of Two Cities,* given the Revolution an air of the stage from which it has never quite been freed. Even Acton, who unfortunately gave his *Lectures on the French Revolution* before Aulard's great collections of documents were fully available, and who, though thinking as a historian, judged as a Catholic, called Robespierre "the most hateful character in the forefront of history since Machiavelli reduced to a code the wickedness of public men". Only since the revaluation of revolutionary history, begun by Aulard and carried on by Mathiez, has it been possible to attempt a more impartial and discriminating estimate of Robespierre and the Revolution.

Paris has never erected a statue to Robespierre: only at Arras, his birthplace, and that amidst fierce controversy, was his bust set up in the *Hôtel de Ville.* In the succession of governments, and in the sway to and fro of public opinion during the century and a half since his death, his name has stood, not for the Fall of the Bastille (commemorated by a statue of Desmoulins in the *Palais-Royal*), nor for the National Assembly (Bailly in the *Jardin du Luxembourg*), nor for the national defence of 1792 (Danton in the *Boulevard Saint-Germain*), but for the Reign of Terror, for the Revolutionary Tribunal, and for the guillotine; and so, with merciless French logic, for the Revolution of 1848 and for the Commune of 1871; a symbol of something that can never be forgotten and whose recurrence may always be feared. But there are a few relics of him in the *Musée Carnavalet,* and (perhaps only because Aulard did him too little honour) a *Société des études Robespierristes* founded by Aulard's successor Mathiez, which has sponsored many useful publications, including collections of Robespierre's *Correspondance* and *Discours,* and a reprint of his periodical *Le Défenseur de la Constitution.*

If a reassessment is to be attempted, on what lines

should it proceed? Under what heads should we examine him: as an orator? as a politician? as a statesman? as a moralist? as a religious thinker?

It would be difficult and controversial to explain and account for the difference between British and French oratory in the eighteenth century. That there was a difference was apparent to English visitors to the National Assembly, and can be felt by readers of the speeches delivered there—not least those of Robespierre. Success as a public speaker was already a normal approach to political leadership in England at this time; and it became so in France, so soon as a French Parliament or "Talking-place" came into being. But in the House of Commons speakers *talked* in language like that they used at the dinner-table or in the club, and *argued* as men expecting to be answered back. In the French assemblies, whose members shared no such club and country-house background, speakers used the technique of the pulpit or the bar; they did not talk, but *spoke;* they did not argue so much as expound; and they were answered (if at all) by counter-expositions. The great orators were those who could read out the best essays in the most effective way. Extemporisation, except in the give and take of personal attack and defence, was remarkably rare. Robespierre, after the attempt to improvise which first made his name, preferred to labour his speeches on paper, as he had done his Academy essays or his pleadings at the Arras bar. He was conscious—too conscious for comfort—of his lack of inches and unimpressive appearance, his weak voice and provincial accent. He would make up for these defects by a sustained seriousness and a carefully studied style, which was reinforced by the thin lips and sharp features of a lawyer and, behind his spectacles (so it seemed to many), the glint of cruel cat-like eyes.

"He would walk slowly to the speaker's desk [says one who saw him]. Almost the only deputy who, in 1794, still dressed and powdered his hair in pre-revolutionary style, he was not unlike a tailor of the old regime. He wore spectacles, perhaps because he really needed them, perhaps to hide the twitchings of his stern and unimpressive features. He started speaking slowly, and his sentences were so long that sometimes, when he paused, and pushed his spectacles up on his forehead, one thought he had nothing more to say: but after looking all round the House, he would pull his spectacles down again, and add a phrase or two to some sentence interrupted and already overlong."

Not an attractive or impressive portrait: and it is evident that Robespierre's oratory was less to the liking of the National Assembly—where he was out of his element except as a minority leader, a party man, or (in the last months) the figure-head of a dictatorial committee—than of the Jacobin Club, which he had re-created in 1791, and where his championship of the *petit bourgeois* and artisan classes, together with his high moral tone and reputation for incorruptible patriotism, won him an unquestioned supremacy. There he was at his ease, and could talk without embarrassment about himself and his ideals; there he could play the patriot, the prophet, and the martyr, sure of sympathy and applause. Other speakers had their admirers too: Mirabeau for strength, Barnave for readiness, Vergniaud for imagination, Danton for homely audacity; but only Robespierre could give full and satisfactory expression to those vague but exciting notions of Liberty, Equality, Justice, and the like whose symbolical figures were beginning to oust the saints and kings of the old regime.

As a politician Robespierre probably had no rival during the Revolution, provided the word to be taken in its narrower sense of a party man, a skilled parliamentarian. His provincial and country town origin, his very ignorance of the world outside the law-courts and Academy of Arras, made it necessary for an ambitious young man to study his new surroundings and colleagues, and to test every foot and hand-hold in his upward ascent. He made it his business to measure personalities, to discover intrigues, to plan policies. By sheer perseverance he made himself into a speaker, and found something to say in the most various debates; the complete list of his speeches runs to 38 in the National Assembly of 1789, 68 in 1790, 77 in 1791, 11 in the Convention of 1792 (he was not a member of the Legislative Assembly), 101 in 1793, and 16 in 1794; whilst at the Jacobin Club he spoke 3 times in 1790, 63 times in 1791, 114 times in 1792, 96 times in 1793, and 47 times in 1794: a total of 634 speeches in five years. Such pertinacity tired and sometimes exasperated his hearers; but it forced them to take him seriously, and to reckon with the support which is always attracted by a politician who knows what he wants and is not afraid of saying so—especially if he habitually opposes the government of the day.

Robespierre, indeed, was made—and he knew it—for opposition rather than for government: he had none of the arts of persuasion or compromise; he could see what should be done, but he could not get men to do it. That was why he was so fatally attracted by the easy way of compulsion, and thought that morality could be taught by intimidation. During all these years he was never out of Paris, except for a few weeks in the autumn of 1791; and his Paris was little more than the few streets between the Tuileries and the Town Hall; he knew no more about the slum dwellers of the East End or the South Bank than he did about the villagers in the Artois country-side. He never learnt how to talk to Duplay's carpenters or to the working men at the street corner. He had many admirers, but few friends, whether in or out of the Assembly and the Club. But he watched and read and questioned; and so acquired, during five years of parliamentary and journalistic life, an unequalled experience of the Revolution and an uncanny insight into the workings of the political machine. The cleverest thing his enemies and rivals ever did was to make him a member of the Committee of Public Safety. In opposition, he destroyed others; in power, he destroyed himself. What they did not foresee was that they would fall with him.

But it is one thing to be a politician and another to be a statesman. Had Robespierre this element of greatness?

If a statesman in time of peace is one who plans and guides the destiny of a nation, if in time of war he is one who inspires and directs the national effort, what can he be in time of revolution? A revolution means the turning upside down of a constitution, a society, a system of values. No individual can inspire or direct more than a part or phase of such a movement. Mirabeau rose to statesmanship in his effort to save the monarchy in 1789–91; Danton in his call to arms and his work for peace in 1792–3. During these years Robespierre was against the monarchy, against the war, against the peace. It cannot be said that his grasp of foreign affairs, of economic problems, or of military matters qualified him to direct these departments of government. His speeches expounding the policy of the Jacobin government were almost wholly concerned with the unmasking and destruction of the "Factions" opposed to it. Only on one subject was he consistent, constructive, and visionary: the Republic of Virtue. Did he become a statesman when in 1793–4 he tried to convert the Jacobin republic into a Calvinistic regime of compulsory virtue and the worship of a Deity who was a Frenchman and a friend of the poor? Let him who will decide.

The inconsistencies of his career are obvious. A pacifist, an anti-militarist, and an opponent of war in 1791, he helped to direct the conquering armies of 1793–4. In 1789 he had shrunk from condemning a criminal to death: four years later he demanded the execution of Louis XVI, claiming that it should be the last; but during the next eighteen months he shared in, and towards the end even directed, the mass murder of hundreds of his fellow-citizens. The question that has to be answered is whether these inconsistencies must be put down to instability of character or to force of circumstances—the first no part of a statesman, the second perhaps something which may excuse lack of statesmanship in time of revolution. As for the war, that was forced upon his party by the Girondins, and he had no alternative but to support it; he salved his pacifist conscience by opposing militarism and insisting on the appointment of "patriot" generals, but he did nothing for international peace. This was perhaps because he found the Home Front, which he studied as a general studies a battlefield, infinitely dangerous, and saw, as Napoleon saw after him, that victory abroad could bring peace at home.

As for the Reign of Terror, it must fairly be said that it was no sudden creation, but a gradual growth, beginning with the popular demand for reprisals on the "criminals" who had shot down "patriots" on August 10, 1792, and with the September Massacre; that the Revolutionary Tribunal had already executed more than fifty people before Robespierre joined the Committee of Public Safety; and that he had no more direct responsibility for the work of the Tribunal than his fellow-dictators. On the other hand, if his signatures to decisions (*arrêtés*) of the Committee are examined (and it is the only evidence available), it appears that of the total of 542 signatures 124 were to *arrêtés* drafted in his own hand, and 47 more signed by himself in the first place, indicating his special responsibility for or interest in the matter concerned; and of these considerably the larger number deal with police matters, especially arrests. It must also be remembered (it was not forgotten at the time) that Robespierre was responsible for the Prairial Law, modelled on his friend Couthon's *Commission d'Orange,* which intensified the Terror, and for the *bureau de police,* which served as a fresh avenue to the guillotine. There can be little hesitation, then, in saying that he developed a predilection for police work, and had only himself to blame if he was held chiefly responsible for the mass executions of 1794.

Yet it was known that he had protected the Girondin deputies imprisoned in 1793, that he needed strong persuasion to sign Danton's death-warrant, and that he had protested against the terrorist measures of Fouché, Carrier, and others. Napoleon, who knew Augustin Robespierre well, often said that Maximilien was not a bloodthirsty man—less so than some other members of the Committee—and that they got rid of him because he contemplated a reversal of their terrorist policy (*"Il a été culbuté parce qu'il voulut devenir modérateur et arrêter la Révolution,"* he told Gourgaud); and there is some corroboration of this in the charges brought against him by his enemies on July 27. What seems clear is that Robespierre, though he may have become cruel, was not naturally inhumane, and that his terrorism was *corruptio optimi pessima,* something that grew out of his very idealism, a moral fanaticism which swept aside common human feelings—the habit of the Inquisitor, who holds that heresy and rebellion are the same sin, and that by sacrifice of the body the soul can be saved.

If this is the explanation of Robespierre's terrorism, the ultimate problem is pushed further back, to his "moralism"—his belief in the ideal state, the Republic of Virtue. What did it mean for him? What validity has it as a mark of statesmanship or a claim to greatness? Here, too, his faith was of gradual growth. He was a son of the professional middle class, with aspirations to gentility and few contacts with the "workers". His belief in the "people" was theoretical, learnt from books, not from experience; he owed it, no doubt, directly or indirectly, to Rousseau, and there is nothing in his correspondence or habits of life to suggest that he moved, except occasionally, outside the *petit bourgeois* atmosphere of the Duplay household, their trade and business acquaintances, the middle-class deputies, and the respectable members of the Jacobin Club. A "republic" meant to him, as it did to most of his young contemporaries, a Roman republic such as he had heard about at school—there was nothing like it in French history—but without any clear constitutional pattern. He was a monarchist until Varennes, a constitutionalist until August 10, a believer in single-party dictatorship after June 1793. He was never, perhaps, a revolutionist at heart, but a radical reformer. His great anxiety was to protect the people from oppression and exploitation by the Government, whether of King and ministers or of Assembly and officials; from injustice, over-taxation, military discipline, illiteracy, and disfran-

chisement. The only basis of a constitution he allowed
was that of human rights.

This belief he expressed once for all in a speech in
the Convention on April 24, 1793.

"The object of every political association [he declared]
is to safeguard the natural and imprescriptible rights of
men, and to develop all their faculties. . . . The most
important rights of men are self-preservation and freedom. . . . These rights belong equally to all men. . . .
Freedom is the right of every man to exercise all his
faculties as he will. Its rule is justice, its limits are the
rights of others, its source is nature, its guarantee is the
law. . . . The law can prohibit only what is harmful and
require only what is useful to society. . . . It is the duty
of society to provide a living for all its members, either
by procuring them work, or by assuring the means of
subsistence to those who are unfit to work. . . . Society
ought to encourage with all its might the progress of
public intelligence, and bring education within the reach
of every citizen. . . . The people is sovereign: the government is its work and its property: public officials are its
agents. . . . Every public position is open to all citizens.
. . . All citizens have an equal right to share in the appointment of the people's deputies, and in legislation."

Some of these ideas were embodied in the Constitution
of 1793—a constitution which remained on the statute-
book but was never enforced; some of them have gradually become part of the common practice of democratic
government; some are still amongst the ideals of the Western world. Belief in the Rights of Man has always been
an act of faith, not a rational conclusion, equality a con-
tradiction of science and experience; but freedom to make
the best of one's life, justice as between man and man,
an opportunity to earn one's living, to be educated, and
to play one's part in the ordering of society—these are
aims acknowledged by every modern state, however much
they may differ as to the best means of attaining them.
The growth of socialism, and the transition from a political to an economic basis of government which have

marked the century and a half since Robespierre announced his programme, vindicate his faith in human nature and justify his claim to stand high amongst the prophets and designers of the Welfare State.

Why, then, did Robespierre's plan fail? One reason, a common reason for such failures, has just been given. He was before his time. Not only was his plan disliked by his associates and inconsistent with their narrower party spirit and lust for political power, but (a more fatal flaw) the country as a whole was not ready for it. Perhaps he only missed his opportunity by a few years. If France had not been at war in 1793, she might have appeased her internal quarrels, assimilated the Revolution, and inaugurated Robespierre's virtuous and enlightened republic; she missed a second opportunity to do so when Napoleon went to war again ten years later. But, on a longer view, Robespierre was half a century too soon. The country had to wait for an industrial revolution to complete its social and political revolution; and that had hardly as yet touched the Continent. In France the Revolution of 1789 had created a new class of small capitalists and landowners whose interests were as conservative as those of the pre-revolutionary aristocracy and *bourgeoisie,* and as hostile to the "workers": the *Loi le Chapelier* prohibiting trades-unionism was not revoked till 1848. It was not till factories, railways, and a Labour Movement gave voice to a new working class that Robespierre's ideals could take shape in a political programme. Modern Russian historians have been taught to deny this *petit bourgeois* idealist a place amongst the founders of international socialism: they will hardly allow any credit even to Marat or Babeuf. But they owe everything to the *bourgeoisie,* and not least to Robespierre, who renounced the privileges of his class to take up the cause of his "social inferiors", and sacrificed his career to the welfare of his country.

There lay behind this a deeper reason for Robespierre's failure. Couthon shared his fear of officialdom, Marat his compassion for the poor, Danton his dislike of religious intolerance, Saint-Just his political philosophy; but none of them could understand or share his religious faith. If they had known their Rousseau better they might have realised how natural a transition his had been from conventional Catholicism through anti-clericalism to the Natural Theism of the *Vicaire Savoyard*. It was a common enough experience in that age. But to make profession of belief in the *Etre Suprème* as the Tutelary God of the French Republic, to admit that poverty alleviated by charity (which they regarded as the inevitable lot of the workers) could be tolerated only if one believed in a benevolent Providence and a life to come, and to expect to unite all religiously minded people in a State-supported worship of God and Immortality— this was more than Robespierre's Jacobin followers, embittered and disillusioned by five years of revolution, could allow. It was not as though it were a mere theory out of which they might have argued him. It was a personal faith, owing something to his Catholic upbringing, something to Rousseau, but most to his concern for the lot of common humanity. He had been "a pretty poor [*assez mauvais*] Catholic", he once admitted, since his school-days; but he revered "the sublime and touching doctrines of virtue and equality that the son of Mary taught to his fellow-citizens". "My God [he wrote on another occasion] is the God who created all men for equailty and happiness; the God who protects the oppressed and punishes the oppressors." Christianity, he thought, preached a morality akin to the political principles of the Revolution, and "if the Declaration of the Rights of Man were torn up by some tyrant, we could rediscover them in the religious law taught by those despots the priests". The religious sentiment, if not the laws of religion, he believed to be "written in every pure and compassionate heart", particularly (he would sometimes say, exclusively) in the hearts of the poor and oppressed. But he made the strange mistake, a mistake only possible for one who had never lived in the country, of supposing that the common people "was not attached to the priest, or to superstition, or to religious ceremonies, but to Christianity as such [*au culte lui-même*]"; and his whole scheme for a State worship was shipwrecked on this fallacy.

Napoleon, the legatee of his failure, and a man without any religious faith, did not make this mistake, and insisted, against the opinion of his secular friends, upon restoring the Catholic Church in its entirety—Pope, priest, and Mass. By posing as a Catholic, he pacified the Vendée, by posing as a Moslem he conquered Egypt, by posing as an Ultramontane he conciliated the Italians; as "the eldest son of the Pope" he carried through the Concordat; if he had remained in Moscow he would have declared for Orthodoxy; if he had crossed the Channel he would have entered London as a good Anglican. Robespierre was utterly incapable of such adaptability; and therefore he failed.

There is something of humanity lacking in the make-up of every Inquisitor. It is not irrelavant to remember, in reckoning the character of Robespierre's political and religious beliefs, the circumstances of his career—that of an orphan with a young family dependent on him, and breathing a narrow middle-class atmosphere; or of an ambitious and hard-working youth, struggling to make a career against the jealousy and dislike of his elders; or of a provincial politician trying to overcome unusual handicaps of appearance, voice, and manner; or of minority opinions cold-shouldered by most of his fellow-members; or of a shyness and awkwardness which drove him from society into a small circle of acquaintances and the solitude of his study. It is not without significance that the only woman with whom he formed any attachment, and that entirely passionless, was the plain and serious-minded Eléonore Duplay.

There is no good reason to suppose, as was sometimes alleged, that Robespierre had Irish blood in him; but it may not be too fanciful to compare his visionary republic with the heaven dreamt of by the mystical priest of *John Bull's Other Island:*

"In my dreams [says *Father Keegan*] it is a country where the State is the Church and the Church the people:

three in one and one in three. It is a commonwealth in which work is play and play is life: three in one and one in three. It is a temple in which the priest is the worshipper and the worshipper the worshipped: three in one and one in three. . . . It is a godhead in which all life is human and all humanity divine: three in one and one in three. It is, in short, the dream of a madman."

Epilogue

THE FRENCH REVOLUTION did not end with the death of Robespierre. It was too big for that. It merely completed its first cycle of development and began its second. Its first had begun in 1789 with a movement—initiated by the privileged classes, guided by the *bourgeoise,* and enforced by the people— against the tyrannical government of a king and a class; after going the round of constitutional monarchy, parliamentary republicanism, and bureaucratic oligarchy, it had ended in another movement, initiated within the Government and enforced from outside it, against the tyranny of a clique. This return to 1789, called the Thermidorian Reaction, took form first in the Constitution of the Year III (1795), an attempt to provide the republican constitution which the Convention had never enacted; but under this again the Directory flouted the Legislature, and after *Fructidor* inaugurated a new tyranny, which the *coup d'état* of *Brumaire* (1799) and the Constitution of the Year VIII transformed into the Napoleonic dictatorship. This second cycle, owing to the able government of Napoleon and the clever way in which he exploited the revolutionary war, could not be ended by any popular movement from within, but only by foreign intervention.

After the return of the Bourbons in 1815, constitutional limits had once more to be imposed upon the reactionary tendencies of Louis XVIII and Charles X, and 1830 found Louis-Philippe almost exactly what Louis XVI was intended to be by the *bourgeois* constitutionalists of 1791. The revolution of 1848—not actually French in origin—repeated many of the phenomena of 1792–4, and ended once more in a tyranny—that of Napoleon III (1851). Again it needed military defeat and invasion to end this third cycle of the Revolution and to inaugurate the Third Republic (1875). This, it may be said with fair confidence, closed the series of cycles that began in

1789; for though the effects of the Revolution are evident in every part of French life today, yet the failure of any political or military adventurer, during a succession of civil crises and *affaires* and the distresses of two world wars, to set up a dictatorship, shows that the French people has become (in its different reading of the words) as deeply attached to liberty and democracy as our own. It is never possible to say for certain—least of all in the present state of the world—that any old movement is over and that no new movement has begun; but the events in France from 1789 to 1875 make a pattern and may fairly be considered as a whole. Within that almost century-long historical sequence there recur the ruling features of the five years 1789–94; and they coincide with and are illustrated by the political career of Robespierre.

How are we to describe this pattern? What estimate are we to make of Robespierre's part in it? What was the real character, the inner meaning, of the Revolution? What is Robespierre's importance in history? A hundred years ago, fifty years ago, it would have been easy to answer both questions to the satisfaction of most readers. In 1853 J. W. Croker contributed to the *Quarterly Review* the last of a series of articles based on his vast collection of revolutionary pamphlets and on his interviews with survivors of the Revolution; they were reprinted a few years later as *Essays on the Early Period of the French Revolution* (1857). Almost at the same moment G. H. Lewes, the husband of George Eliot, published his *Life of Maximilien Robespierre* (1849). Both books reflected the new views of the Revolution and Robespierre that had come into French literature as a result of the political events of 1830 and 1848—the first crisis reviving interest in the constitutional monarchy of 1789–91, the second rehabilitating the Girondin-Jacobin republic of 1792–4. It was now possible to idealise the Girondins with Lamartine (1847), or the Jacobins with Louis Blanc (1847), or the French people with Michelet (1847–53); Robespierre was no longer either a bloodthirsty tyrant or a "sea-green Incorruptible", but a political fanatic, with an excess both of good and bad qualities. Yet such views took a long time to spread, and the common idea of the Revolution remained for many years that embodied in two of the most popular books of the age—Carlyle's *French Revolution* (1837) and Dickens' *Tale of Two Cities* (1859): the Revolution was still identified with the Reign of Terror, and Robespierre was still supposed to be a dictator who sent his rivals to the guillotine.

Fifty years ago the scene had changed. Sorel (1885) had brought the Revolution into relation with European history, and Aulard had begun (1889) the publication of the records of the Jacobin Club and the Committee of Public Safety, together with a series of works which for the first time applied to the Revolution the scientific methods of historical criticism. When Morse Stephens published his (unfinished) *History of the French Revolution* (1891), and Lord Acton delivered (1895) his *Lectures on the French Revolution,* it was possible for the first time to give an accurate and balanced view of the Revolution considered as a political movement. There still remained two aspects which were not yet fully realised —the economic background, and the part played by the class-interests both of *bourgeoisie* and workers; these inquiries were attempted in Jaurès' *Histoire socialiste* (1901–4) and in numerous works by his editor (1922) Mathiez, whose militant Robespierrism inspired a fresh approach to the revolutionary period, both in England and America.

The present-day historian, with so much experience and so many experiments behind him, must not suppose that he can deliver a final judgment. Neither he nor his age is exempt from partiality and prejudice. But he is able to say that most of the country he has to describe has been mapped, many of the rivers traced to their sources, the mountain-heights roughly estimated, and routes driven through the less accessible districts. It would be possible now, as it would not have been fifty years ago, to *chronicle* the French Revolution in terms to which every historian, in proportion as he studied the subject, would be bound to agree. But to write a *history* of the Revolution requires something less of describing and something more of thinking. For, whatever may be said, all happenings are not of equal importance, all personages of equal significance, all laws and institutions of equal influence upon the course of society; and though the historian must disclaim any divine insight into the order of the world, or any power of detailed prophecy, yet his work will remain without value or interest unless he tries to find the texture beneath the surface of the tapestry and the pattern upon it. For where human will and passion are at work there must be a pattern, however confused and difficult to unravel.

Let a man, then, put aside, so far as he can, preconceived opinions about the French Revolution, and try to think himself back into Paris and France as they were in 1789, into the course of events as it has been reconstructed by six generations of historians, into the ideas and purposes of those who played the leading parts in the drama; and let him then consider how much of all this was of lasting effect in France, or contributed to the history and ideas of the Western world.

The first thing to occur to anyone studying the Revolution from this point of view will probably be the obvious but too often overlooked reflection that it was a *French* revolution. Though prefaced by the political and social programmes of the Enlightenment in Prussia, Russia, Austria, and Tuscany, and encouraged by the sympathy and help that France had given to the North American "rebels", it was a native and national movement which owed little to anything going on elsewhere in the world. Though many of the ideas propounded by its leaders, and some of the institutions to which it gave birth, were of English or American origin, yet neither the Encyclopædists nor Rousseau would have turned a monarchy into a republic or a political reformation into a social-economic revolution. The Nobility began it, the *bourgeoisie* carried it on, the agriculturists gave it national backing; yet the power of Paris which lay behind all the crucial developments of the movement was not due to any isolated class rising of the "workers", but to their temporary and local solidarity with the tradesmen, shop-keepers, journalists, and other discontented classes of the city. This community of feeling was exploited by politicians and agitators; but these "leaders" were, for the most part, singularly unleaderlike; their reputations seldom lasting overnight, with few principles or policies, weather-cock heroes (*girouettes*) most of them, swung by any change in the wind of popular favour. This was not the form that revolution had taken in England or in America; it would contribute little to the pattern of revolution in Russia, or Germany, or South America. It was characteristically French. It was determined throughout by the geographical, racial, and cultural unity of France, which still survived beneath the surface of provincial and class privilege; by the universal influence, however thinly diffused, of the Catholic Church; by the lingering respect of the people, however disillusioned, for the Bourbon monarchy; by the centripetal pull of Paris upon the economic and intellectual resources of the country; and by consciousness of the Rhine frontier, so much more real to the national mind than the Atlantic seaboard.

The second point that will probably occur to a reflective reader is that it was primarily not a political and constitutional but a social and economic revolution. The things that catch the eye are no doubt the summoning of a parliament, the deposition and execution of a king, the declaration of a republic, the strife of political parties, and the common massacre of their leaders; or perhaps the abolition of feudal rights, the secularisation of the Church, the institution of popular elections. Some of these political and constitutional changes were modified or revised within a few years, but fundamental changes remained: the idea that all Frenchmen were fellow-citizens (*citoyens*) with equal rights before the judge, the tax-collector, and the recruiting officer; the co-partnership of landlord, farmer, and labourer in the ownership of the soil, which gave political stability to a country predominantly agricultural; a government founded on popular election (however indirectly, and with whatever distrust in its elected representatives); and a culture broadly based on a new interest in life and a national system of education. Real revolutions are like that. Politicians may invent new laws, generals may inflict or suffer defeats, authors may propound new philosophies, and preachers bring their faiths up to date; but social, economic, and moral changes are going on below the surface, in the manners and notions of everyday folk, which are not realised until it is all over; and then they are beyond control:

> *Experience shows that planned reforms*
> *Are great, but those unplanned are greater.*

What the Revolution did for France was, superficially, to transform a monarchy into a republic, class privilege into political equality, and arbitrary government into the rule of law; what it did fundamentally was to create a French nation, French patriotism, an intelligent and well-to-do as well as (what it always was) a thrifty working class, and (not so good) an aristocracy of wealth and talent disdainful, as the old aristocracy of birth had been, of the business of government.

In an empty world this new France, with its happy balance of land, people, and institutions, might have become the Utopia of Robespierre's dream: *O majesté d'un grand peuple heureux par le suel sentiment de sa force, de sa gloire, et de sa vertu!*

In an empty world. But the world was not empty—of territorial greed, of economic rivalry, of fear of republicanism; and the new nation was dragged before it was ready into foreign war, civil strife, political quarrels, party tyranny, and terrorism; only to be rescued from disaster by a military distatorship, which altered the original pattern of its democracy, and enabled it to survive, changed, in a crowded and changing world. For Napoleon, half a foreigner and a Jacobin "careerist", was above all a soldier, with a strategic eye and a parade-ground love of order; and though the Empire lost all the territory that the Republic had won, yet it provided for the democratic institutions which the people had chosen in 1789 and yet had never quite assimilated, a stiffening of law and administration which the Revolution had failed to create—a defensive covering for the sensitive organism within.

It may always remain doubtful—for history has instances pointing either way—whether a nation influences the world more in victory or in defeat, whether it is better for civilisation that it should "rise" or "fall". But it is certain that France of the fifteenth to the eighteenth centuries provided a rich soil for the flowering of seeds of art brought from Italy, of philosophy from England, of liberty from America, and that these flowers have, since the Revolutionary and Napoleonic age, been transplanted and taken on new forms in every part of the world. There is no democracy but owes something to the "ideas of 1789", no charter of liberty that is not based on the Declaration of Rights, no programme of social services that does not borrow from the work of the National Assemblies. Finally, there is no idealistic or irresolute government which may not profitably study the fall of the Girondins, no dictatorship that should not be warned by the destruction of Jacobinism, and no political moralist and reformer who might not take to heart the sad confession which Robespierre, on second thoughts, erased from his last speech in public: "But for my conscience, I should be the unhappiest man alive" (*Otez-moi ma conscience, je serais le plus malheureuz de tous les hommes*).

Index